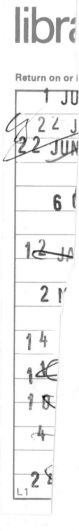

Perspectives on a Decade of Small Business Research

Bolton Ten Years On

edited by
JOHN STANWORTH
AVA WESTRIP
Small Business Unit,
Polytechnic of Central London
DAVID WATKINS
New Enterprise Centre,
Manchester Business School
and
JOHN LEWIS
Management Studies Department,
University of Glasgow

Gower

Published by
Gower Publishing Company Limited,
Gower House, Croft Road, Aldershot,
Hampshire GU11 3HR, England

and

Gower Publishing Company,
Old Post Road, Brookfield,
Vermont 05036, U.S.A.

Reprinted 1984, 1986

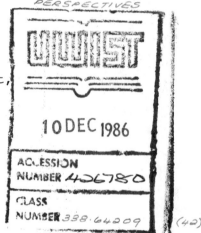

British Library Cataloguing in Publication Data

Perspectives on a decade of small business
    research: Bolton ten years on
    1. Small business - Great Britain - Congresses
    I. Stanworth, John
    338.6'42'0941   HD2346.G7

    ISBN 0-566-00587-5

Printed and bound in Great Britain by
Antony Rowe Ltd, Chippenham, Wiltshire

Contents

Editors and authors

MICHAEL BEESLEY is Professor of Economics at the London Business School.

PAUL CHAPLIN is a free-lance lecturer currently attached to the New Enterprise Centre, Manchester Business School.

MICHAEL CROSS is a Senior Research Fellow at the Technical Change Institute, London. He was previously a Research Fellow at the Durham University Business School.

JAMES CURRAN is Reader in Industrial Sociology, Kingston Polytechnic.

FRANK GREENHOW was, until his recent retirement, Project Manager - Small Businesses, National Westminster Bank Limited.

JOE HORNER is a Tax Adviser with Kidsons Chartered Accountants.

JENSINE HOUGH is a Research Officer, Small Business Unit, Polytechnic of Central London.

DAVID KIRBY is a Senior Lecturer in Geography at St. David's University College, University of Wales.

JOHN LEWIS is a Lecturer in Production Management, University of Glasgow.

ALISTAIR RAINNIE is a Research Officer in the School of Occupational Studies, Newcastle-on-Tyne Polytechnic.

MICHAEL SCOTT is a Principal Lecturer in the School of Occupational Studies, Newcastle-on-Tyne Polytechnic.

JOHN STANWORTH is Professor of Management Studies and Director - Small Business Unit, Polytechnic of Central London.

DAVID WATKINS is Director - New Enterprise Centre, Manchester Business School.

JEAN WATKINS is a research worker associated with the New Enterprise Centre, Manchester Business School.

AVA WESTRIP is a Research Officer, Small Business Unit, Polytechnic of Central London.

PETER WILSON is a Senior Research Officer, Small Business Unit, London Business School.

Acknowledgements

The editors would like to thank all authors whose papers appear in this book for their generous contributions of time and effort and the speed with which they responded to editorial requests in the preparation of their papers. In recognition of special efforts associated with the task of book production, special mention is due to James Curran, Kingston Polytechnic, Betty Elliott and Jensine Hough, Polytechnic of Central London and Philip Dowell, London Business School.

Preface

I congratulate Professor John Stanworth, his colleagues of the Polytechnic of Central London and members of the UKSBMTA connected with a
most successful research conference held in November 1981 from which
this impressive collection of research papers on the small business
field has been compiled.

The major difficulty faced by the Committee of Inquiry on Small Firms
during its deliberations in 1969-71 was the almost complete absence of
research information into the small firm sector at that time.   We
commissioned eighteen Research Reports, mostly prepared by outside
academic and consultant groups, but recognised that, despite the
essential contribution which these reports made to our conclusions, we
were still 'barely scratching the surface' of a vitally important
economic area - comprising as it did some 25 per cent of the employed
population and 20 per cent of GNP and, perhaps more importantly,
representing the seedbed of our industrial and commercial structure of
the future.

Moreover, in order to reduce our task to manageable proportions we
deliberately omitted detailed study of important areas such as agriculture and the professions.   To recall:

> 'We felt that since the special problems of these industries
> have already been studied in detail, either by the respons-
> ible departments of Government or by powerful professional
> associations, we should be unable to add much to knowledge
> about these activities.   However, the small units in
> these sectors are businesses in their own right, and they
> share many of the common problems of the small firms in
> those areas of industry and commerce which we have studied
> in some depth.   To the extent that they do so, our findings
> are relevant to their position.   In many other instances
> our examination of specialised trades and sub-trades has
> been sketchy, although we have endeavoured to include their
> activities in our statistical analyses.'

Subsequent developments, particularly in the service industries, and the new phenomenon of inter-city blight have meant that these areas which we omitted from our own studies, offer important research opportunities and I am delighted that some of the papers in this symposium are addressed at remedying the gap.

One conclusion which emerged from our studies of Britain's overseas competitors was that those economies which had a strong small firm sector - e.g. USA (ten times as many small firms as in the UK) or Germany (40 per cent or nearly 500,000 more) or Japan where small firms accounted for some 60 per cent of employment and 50 per cent of GNP - and which also had an overt policy of Government support towards small firms, were consistently growing at a more rapid rate than the UK economy. Many of these competitor countries also had evolved a Government coordinated research effort into their own small firm sector. We still lack this impetus and focal point and it is most encouraging that despite this 'benign neglect' in the UK, individual academics, encouraged by their institutions and the UKSBMTA, have achieved so much with so little official support.

A great deal more remains to be done before we can really develop a concerted national policy towards the small firms sector which will encourage - and even permit - small firms to play the crucial role in our economy of which they are capable and which they alone can perform - whether it be in creating new and real employment opportunities, developing the new technology products and industries of the next two decades, or regenerating our inner cities and declining regions and creating a more resilient and balanced industrial and commercial structure for the future.

Certain private initiatives are afoot to launch Research Institutes or Foundations to sponsor further work in the small firm sector, and I applaud these developments. I hope that this innovative publication by the UKSBMTA will add momentum and encouragement to this vitally important field of study.

JOHN BOLTON

Introduction

In July 1969, the late Anthony Crosland, then President of the Board of
Trade, set up a Committee of Inquiry on Small Firms.   It was to be
chaired by John Bolton and its principal terms of reference were 'to
consider the role of small firms in the national economy and the
problems confronting them'.   The Committee submitted its report in
September 1971 and what is now commonly known as the Bolton Report was
published two months later in November.   It was accompanied by eighteen
research reports specially commissioned by the Committee, concerned
with a wide range of aspects of small business operation.

The Report marked a turning point in attitudes to the small enterprise
in Britain arriving, as it did, at the tail end of a period in which
the notion that economic salvation in an advanced industrial society
was inextricably linked with large size had led to what many have seen
as serious distortions in the structure of our economy.   The Committee's
sceptical examination of this notion coincided with emerging doubts
about the benefits of large size among politicians, academics and the
public at large.   Many official Committee of Inquiry reports are soon
forgotten, even by specialists in the relevant area, but the Bolton
Report remains remarkably influential among all those interested in the
small business.

Virtually every contribution to the mushrooming body of small
business research takes the Bolton Report's observations and findings
as its starting point.   Bankers and politicians have closely followed
its recommendations in developing their own strategies and policies
towards the small business.   It has helped lead to a climate of small
enterprise consciousness where nearly every academic business school
and management department has its small business specialists and enter-
price development programmes.   Television and press coverage of small

business affairs has reached levels undreamt of in 1971 and publishers clamour to add small business titles to their lists.

The 1981 UKSBMTA Small Business Research Conference, from which the papers in this book are drawn, celebrated the 10th anniversary of the publication of the Bolton Report and took as its theme an assessment of the influence of the Committee's work on thinking and research on the small enterprise over the past ten years. The pioneering efforts of the Committee, particularly in terms of establishing the conceptual groundwork and highlighting the key issues requiring further attention, are widely recognised and amply illustrated by the papers in this volume.

What is also revealed by the papers is the great variety and vigour to be found in small business research in Britain at the moment. It is rare to see such a multi-disciplinary effort, involving a large number of independent researchers focusing on varied aspects of the same area of economic activity. Yet in the years since 1971 this is almost precisely what has happened with the closest resemblance to the kind of research 'blitzkrieg' characteristic of U.S. research in the behavioural and management sciences that we could expect to see. The debt to John Bolton and his colleagues for their part in the remarkable process is enormous.

The papers in this volume reflect two main aims. First, they attempt to follow through some of the areas of interest identified in the Bolton Report as being crucial to the small business sector in Britain. Here we are thinking of issues such as finance, taxation, training, industrial relations and especially the central question of government aid for the small enterprise. Second, a number of the papers are concerned with issues which were not considered by the Committee or which have only assumed a growing importance since 1971. Here we refer to the papers on such topics as producer co-operatives, franchising, women in business and the entrepreneurial base of the large firm. It is this second group of papers which so clearly indicates just how much small business research has been confidently developing since Bolton.

The selection of papers for this volume was not easy and, inevitably, we would have liked to include others also presented at the Conference. We should like to thank the authors of the papers included for the

prompt revision and editing of their contributions which has allowed
us to get this collection into print so quickly. The Bolton Committee,
through their Report, stimulated small business research in Britain
enormously and the papers in this volume are proudly presented a
decade later as a salute to their pioneering efforts. We believe that
the quality of the work in the papers presented in this volume fully
lives up to those early efforts.

John Stanworth
Ava Westrip
David Watkins
John Lewis

I BOLTON TEN YEARS ON

Bolton Ten Years On — A Research Inventory and Critical Review
JAMES CURRAN AND JOHN STANWORTH

In November 1971, the Report of the Committee of Inquiry on Small Firms
- better known as the Bolton Report - was published.   The influence of
the Report on thinking about the role of the small firm in Britain over
the last decade would be difficult to overstate.   It aroused intense
interest among politicians, academics and the media and its findings
and recommendations have formed the bedrock of virtually all research,
analysis and policy making since.

Academic interest in the small enterprise has increased in the subsequent decade to a level where few business schools or management
departments dare be without their small business specialists and small
business courses.   These activities have been supported by a rapidly
expanding body of research, based on inputs from several disciplines,
covering many aspects of small enterprise operations.   The research
literature ranges from the highly theoretical through to well-designed
empirical studies.   Each has informed the other to produce one of the
most remarkable examples of sustained academic exploration of business
activity yet seen in Britain.

Prior to Bolton, the sparse literature on the small firm was over-
whelmingly American in origin.   'Classic' studies such as those of
Collins et al (1964), Mayer and Goldstein (1961) and key theoretical
contributions such as that of McClelland (1961) all fall into this
category.   While this literature was often uncritically accepted in
Britain, this was not particularly serious since interest in the small
enterprise was limited.   Big was still seen as beautiful and growth was
seen as the key to the treasures of increased economies of scale.

Faced with a dearth of research on the small firm in Britain, the Bolton Committee commissioned several pieces of research which subsequently resulted in eighteen research reports (the Bolton Report, 1971, Appendix III). These can be seen as the beginnings of a research revival in the area, though, in fact, some of the most influential studies in the field were being conducted concurrently (Ingham, 1970; Boswell, 1973; Batstone, 1975, for example). Given the pioneering task undertaken by the Bolton Committee and the constraints typically associated with commissioned research, it is not surprising that, to an academic audience ten years later, the Committee's research coverage and methodology appear, on occasions, somewhat patchy.

For instance, the Report showed that small firms employed a substantial proportion of the labour force - over 30 per cent of the workers in the industries covered by the enquiry (Bolton Report, 1971: 33). Yet not a single piece of research directly investigated employer-employee relations or employee reactions to employment in the small firm. The Committee's two principal surveys enquiring into the characteristics of small firms in Britain achieved response rates of only 13 and 22 per cent and most of the various research reports make little attempt to claim to be more than preliminary studies.

Nevertheless, the report carried out the vital task of bringing together a corpus of propositions that formed the conventional view of the small enterprise as a socio-economic entity throughout the 1970s. Ten years on, it is appropriate to return to these concerns and see how later research and thinking supports or questions them.

SMALL FIRMS: CONCEPTUALISATIONS AND STATISTICS

Two basic questions discussed at length in the Bolton Report were the conceptualisation of the small firm as a socio-economic entity and the size of the small firm population in Britain. The answers given to these questions have remained influential, albeit controversial, and contemporary discussion regrettably shows little real advance on either.

The Committee initially conceptualised the small enterprise in terms of a qualitative trichotomous notion stressing small market share, personalised management and independence of decision-making (Bolton Report, 1971: 1-2). They immediately ran up against problems of converting their notion into quantitative indicators suitable for empirical research. Their solution - the adoption of non-comparable numerical definitions for each of the nine sectors of economic activity covered by the inquiry has had considerable influence on thinking and research since (Bolton Report, 1971: 3).

But for the main sector with which the Committee was concerned - manufacturing - it is now widely recognised that the upper size limit adopted of 200 employees was probably rather high.   Research being conducted contemporaneously to the Committee's work generally adopted an upper limit of 100 employees (Batstone, 1969:   10;   Ingham, 1970: 65) and some researchers who adopted a similar definition to the Committee, have since expressed doubts on this (for example, Curran and Stanworth, 1979b: 428).   Whether similar doubts should be expressed about the definitions for the other eight sectors is less certain since there has been little subsequent research, but certainly inflation has meant problems for the monetary definitions adopted for the motor trades, wholesale trades and miscellaneous sectors.

It might have been expected that researchers in allied areas such as organisation studies would have contributed to the clarification of these problems.   But, unfortunately, they have virtually neglected qualitative conceptualisations (Kimberly, 1976) and their quantitative conceptualisations have developed little beyond a further clarification of the limitations of this kind of approach (Agarwal, 1979;   Gupta, 1980). In fact, the majority of discussions of size in organisational studies throughout the 1970s assumed pan-industrial quantitative conceptualisations, neglecting the very point established by the Bolton Report in its opening paragraphs: that particular industries will have considerable variations in their combinations of numbers of employees, assets and turnover so that no single numerical indicator can serve as a universal quantitative conceptualisation of 'small'.

The rather obvious alternative of attempting to combine qualitative and quantitative approaches into a single conceptualisation has attracted few theorists in the 1970s. One reason for this is that most organisational theorists interested in size aspects have almost exclusively concentrated on structural aspects (Kimberly, 1976;   Pugh and Hickson, 1976;   Pugh and Hinings, 1976).   In practice, this has meant largely relating one numerical measure (size) to another (the number of levels

5

of authority in the organisation, the ratio of the administrative component to other components in the organisation and so on) with little, if any, reference to qualitative aspects of the organisation.

In short, the gulf between qualitative and quantitative conceptualisations of the small firm so clearly established by the Bolton Report has remained unbridged in the ensuing decade. In practice, however, small firm researchers often pragmatically combine their selected size indicators with qualitative elements relative to the specific context of their research. For example, community character (Batstone, 1975), economic sector (Bechhofer et al, 1974), industrial sub-culture (Newby et al, 1978; Curran and Stanworth, 1979b) and national culture (Bechhofer and Elliott, 1981) have all been used in the analysis of small enterprises initially defined numerically. For the moment this rather unsystematic approach will apparently have to continue to serve researchers.

This leads us back to the consideration of statistics on the small firm since the Bolton Report. Employing its nine quantitative indicators, the Report concluded that there were around 820,000 small firms employing 4.4 million or about 30 per cent of the labour force in the sectors covered (Bolton Report, 1976: 33-34). But, as the Report also pointed out, the Committee had omitted other small business activity accounting for around a further 430,000 enterprises employing a further 1.6 million people.

The sectors not covered included agricultural enterprises, of which a high proportion would be described as 'small' by most observers and many kinds of financial and personal services. For example, most estate agents, insurance brokers, accountants, general practitioners, dentists and legal practitioners are in small partnerships. Leaving aside agriculture, the neglect of these other areas could be seen as a rather backward-looking view. The essential character of advanced industrial societies is that they are shifting their major economic emphasis from manufacturing to various kinds of tertiary activities (Galbraith, 1969; Bell, 1974; Gershuny, 1978) so we might have expected a grater concern with these areas of the economy.

The numerical picture of the small enterprise in Britain in 1981 appears no clearer now than ten years ago. Indeed, in some respects it is becoming less clear. Small businessmen have always been reluctant to provide even elementary statistical data for the Census of Production and other official information gathering exercises. National government is the only body with the resources and the authority to collect such information but politicians have become increasingly afraid of offending small businessmen with 'unnecessary' paperwork and, more recently, the wish to reduce public expenditure has been used to rationalise collecting less information on the small enterprise.

The Wilson Committee, reporting in March 1979 - which incidentally recommended a small Department of Industry statistical unit to collect and coordinate data on small firms (Wilson Report, 1979: 38) - selected only three sectors in which to estimate changes since 1971. In manufacturing, between 1963 and 1973 (then the most recently available data), the number of small firms had increased from 66,000 to 74,000. As Table 1 shows, more recent Census of Production data indicates that there were 87,000 small manufacturing enterprises in 1978. Between 1963 and 1973 the proportion of the manufacturing labour force employed in small firms fell from 21.3 per cent to 20.7 per cent. For 1978, Census of Production data, based on establishments, suggests a figure of 22.8 per cent.

This data has to be treated with great caution because of the difficulties involved in gathering statistics in this area, including changes in the basis of collection. But the conclusion drawn by the Wilson Committee - which seems borne out by more recent data - was that the number of small manufacturing firms has increased since 1971 with their share of the labour force and output being more or less maintained.

The other two economic sectors discussed by the Wilson Committee were retailing and construction. They concluded that small firms in retailing had continued to decline and the decline showed signs of accelerating (Wilson Report, 1979: 48-49). In construction, the statistics were again far from satisfactory. For example, an additional 25,000 firms were identified and added to the list in 1973 and further changes in data collecting were expected to lead to the 'discovery' of more small firms in this sector (Wilson, 1979: 50), but the proportion of small to large firms had apparently stayed broadly constant during the 1970s period for which data was available.

TABLE 1

SMALL ENTERPRISE DATA, MANUFACTURING INDUSTRIES, UK, 1963-1978

	No. of Small Enterprises (thousands)	As % of All Enterprises	Employment in Small Enterprises as % of Total	Net Output (by Value) of Small Enterprises as % of Total
1963	65.7	94.1	21.3	18.0
1968	66.1	94.9	20.8	18.1
1970	70.9	95.2	21.3	18.5
1971	71.4	95.3	21.0	17.9
1972	69.0	95.4	21.5	18.4
1973	74.1	95.7	20.7	17.1
1974	81.1	96.0	21.5*	17.7*
1975	83.4	96.3	21.9*	18.0*
1976	86.3	96.5	22.6*	18.2*
1977	86.7	96.6	22.5*	18.7*
1978	87.2	96.7	22.8*	19.3*

Because the distribution of manufacturing firms is highly skewed, a definition of 'small' as firms employing less than 100 would not proportionately alter these figures. For example, in 1977 enterprises employing less than 100 were 94.5% of all manufacturing enterprises and in 1978, 93.8%. They employed 17.1%* of all manufacturing workers in 1977 and 17.3%* in 1978. They contributed 14.0%* of net manufacturing output in 1977 and 14.4%* in 1978.

Notes: 'Small' is defined as an enterprise employing less than 200 persons.
*Data based on establishment not enterprise figures.

Sources: Interim Report of the Committee to Review the Functioning of Financial Institutions, Cmnd. 7503, HMSO 1979, Tables 2.1, 2.2 and 2.3. Reports of the Censuses of Production, 1974-75, 1976, 1977 and 1978, all published HMSO, 1978-81.

A broad picture of the small firm in three sectors of the economy is insufficient to arrive at any generalisation about either the relative position of the small firm in Britain or changes in its position since 1971. The lack of accurate data is a profound disadvantage for researchers but it is even more serious for policy makers. Successive Governments have developed policies for encouraging small firms and argued that they have a central role in the reshaping of Britain's economy yet, at the same time, the statistical base required for rational policy making is being dismantled or allowed to wither away.

Overall, therefore, the statistical picture of the significance of
the small firm in Britain's economy in 1981 is, if anything, less clear
than in 1971.   But, to be fair, even if an adequate, properly staffed
government statistical unit was set up, there would still be difficulties in arriving at an accurate and comprehensive view.   Small firms are
a constantly changing population and, as we discuss below, a substantial
but unknown number, exist in the half world between the legal and the
illegal.   Both researchers and policy makers deserve and need a better
data base on the small enterprise and this should be a matter for urgent
government action.

OTHER FORMS OF SMALL BUSINESS ENTERPRISE

The Bolton Report took a rather conventional view of the small business,
concentrating on manufacturing and distribution enterprises of the
traditional variety.   In the 1970s we became more aware of varieties
of small enterprise not discussed by Bolton, whose contribution to the
economy is gradually being recognised as being of considerable significance.   To illustrate this we can refer to just two such varieties of
economic activity, franchising and the so-called 'black economy' (for
an example of a third area, see the paper on Co-operatives by Paul
Chaplin later in this volume).

A rapid expansion of franchising in Britain has occurred since 1971
though important areas of the economy have long been dominated by the
franchise format, most notably brewing and car and petroleum distribution.   Essentially, franchising consists of an organisation (the
franchisor) with a market tested business package, centred on a product
or service, establishing contractual relationships with franchisees
(typically, aspiring small businessmen) who set up their own business to
operate under the franchisor's trade name and market the product or
service in the manner specified.

The central characteristic of the franchised business is the special
relationship existing between companies where the central aim of one of
the companies is to promote the existence of a large number of smaller,
satellite enterprises.   The main advantages to the franchisor are the
rapid achievement of national coverage for his product or service with
most of the capital put up by others (the franchisees) and the

elimination of many of the motivational and personnel problems which increasingly arise where face to face customer contact occurs at a large number of outlets remote from head office.

Given that our economy is moving towards a greater emphasis on tertiary activities, it is also moving towards being a service economy highly suited to franchising. It is not surprising, therefore, that franchising in Britain appears to have undergone a substantial expansion in the 1970s although exact figures are hard to come by.

Franchise World, the industry's trade magazine, currently lists over sixty franchises on offer in Britain, ranging from the long established Wimpy fast food operation which now has approaching 600 outlets in Britain alone, to examples of the more recent trend of major companies converting some of their operations to a franchised form. Among the latter are Trust Houses Forte and the British School of Motoring.

The British Franchise Association, to which most of the major franchisors in Britain belong, claimed that its members had over 4,000 outlets in operation by the end of 1980 and that expansion was occurring at around 10 per cent a year. Most of these outlets have been set up since the early 1970s. To this total might be added the 13,000 independently owned petrol service stations who operate in association with one or other of the major oil companies (Institute of Petroleum, 1980) and the 7,500 franchised car dealerships (Motor Agents' Association, 1981). Around thirty-five thousand tenanted public houses (Brewers' Society, 1981) could also be included since the tenant brewer relationship is often seen as the earliest kind of franchise in a modern day context. Finally, it is possible to add voluntary grocery wholesale-retail franchises such as Spar, Mace, VG, etc. and similar operations which have recently emerged in photographic retailing.

It is impossible to put an exact figure on the number of franchised enterprises in Britain but our estimate is around 80,000. A not insignificant number of these have come into existence since 1971 and represent a net addition to the number of small enterprises in Britain. We expect this trend to continue both in the form of new operations and existing businesses converting to the franchise form. In other words, official statistics seem to suggest a continued decline in the conventional small business but to take this as a firm indication of a decline in the small business in Britain generally is to ignore these recent developments in the economy.

This is further underlined when we shift attention from the legitimate to the illegitimate, the 'black economy', taking this to refer to the production of goods and services for gain which is systematically concealed from official notice in order to avoid the payment of tax or other dues to the State. The black economy was not discussed by Bolton and it is unclear whether it was important in the late 1960s but it is obvious that it has become very important since. Estimates vary but a recent analysis argued that it might be worth as much as 15 per cent of the national income, equivalent to unpaid taxes of around £9 billion a year (Feige, 1981).

Undoubtedly, the major impetus to the development of the black economy was the introduction of VAT in 1973 which taxed a whole range of hitherto untaxed services and activities and promoted wholesale evasion. Other factors which have been suggested as playing an influence have been increasing levels of National Insurance contributions, employment protection legislation and technological change (Gershuny and Pahl, 1980). For instance, in several kinds of activity such as building maintenance and decoration, new tools and methods have made it easier for the unskilled to offer their services ("for cash") and consumers have shifted their allegiance from conventional suppliers to these new sources.

A large proportion of the black economy is small business activity even if of an illegitimate kind. Some will consist of legitimate small businesses becoming illegitimate and some will be the seeds of tomorrow's legitimate small businesses; having expanded within the black economy they become big enough (and visible enough) to register and trade officially. But many of these enterprises will remain outside official knowledge forever. Overall, the black economy is now an established part of our economy as a whole and represents an important outlet for entrepreneurial talent.

We would not want to enter a dispute on the exact number of small firms in Britain or whether this number is increasing or decreasing - the data are simply too imprecise. The official data suggest only a moderate decline in the 1970s and against this we have noted a number of counter trends. The fashionable vogue for bigness so prevalent in the 1960s has long been reversed. Economists who stressed economies of

scale in the past now balance this with an equal emphasis on the dis-
economies involved. Concentration in many sectors is not increasing
rapidly (Lawson, 1981) and aspects of new technology from plastics to
microprocessors, are highly suited to small scale production. Overall,
therefore, we would argue that the small enterprise sector is as healthy
in 1981 as in 1971, despite the onset of the severest recession since
the 1930s.

THE OWNER-MANAGER AND THE ENTREPRENEUR

The characterisation of the small businessman offered in the Bolton
Report was uni-dimensional. The Committee's researchers talked to a lot
of small businessmen but largely took them at their own estimation.
This self-estimation saw the small business owner-manager disadvantaged
by politicians, banks, large companies and local authorities, and mis-
understood by the general public. Making ends meet was a perpetual
nightmare demanding virtually a total commitment of time and energy for
barely adequate rewards. Trade unions were seen as another 'threat'
despite the fact that 'their' workers really wanted nothing to do with
unions. Getting skilled, loyal workers was increasingly difficult,
even though inside the enterprise relations between boss and worker were
seen as being warm and friendly.

Ten years later, research on the owner-manager and the entrepreneur
offers a more rounded picture with rather more warts though carrying
substantially more conviction. As Bolton suggested, small firm owner-
managers are far from randomly drawn from the population (Bolton Report,
1971: 22-25). They tend to be relatively poorly educated and often
running a small business is an alternative to conventional forms of
achievement in society. This is increasingly equated with high office
in a large organisation and has become greatly dependent upon qualifications in our credentialist society. For those who, for some reason,
fail to obtain such qualifications, a small business is a major alternative path to success.

It has been suggested that a new kind of entrepreneur emerged in the
1970s - the 'R and D' or 'Highway 128' entrepreneur as he has sometimes
been labelled. He has had an extended education, perhaps to PhD level,
in science or engineering and especially in some area of new technology.

He has also realised that his special knowledge can be converted into the basic asset of a new enterprise. This technological entrepreneur received considerable attention in the United States in the early 1970s (see, for example, Lyles, 1974). But whether he has emerged to any marked extent in Britain is doubtful (Belbin, 1980).

One finding in the Bolton Report (1971: 23) which has been reiterated again and again, is that few owner-managers make financial gain their key goal. Without exception, studies of entrepreneurs and owner-managers in the 1970s all underline this point (Boswell, 1973; Stanworth and Curran, 1973; Scase and Goffee, 1981; Bannock, 1981: 36-38). Equally, the findings indicate the tremendous stress placed on autonomy and independence as a major personal goal, with the enterprise as the major arena for its expression.

These findings also accord with the main ideas emerging in the recent revival of theorising and research into the petit bourgeoisie (Bechhofer and Elliott, 1976, 1978 and 1981). This 'inbetween' class in modern industrial society had been rather neglected but it is now becoming accepted that they continue to survive and may even be increasing in number. Echoing the idea of the small businessman as socially marginal (Stanworth and Curran, 1973) this recent literature emphasises the continuing vulnerability of the petit bourgeoisie to change, booms, recessions and political decisions. Yet their great resilience as a stratum (Goldthorpe, Llewellyn and Payne, 1980) against formidable economic and political odds, fully reflects the striving for autonomy in their psychological make-up.

In turn, these psychological characteristics of entrepreneurs and small firm owner-managers manifest themselves in a distinct managerial style. Kets de Vries (1977) in a summary of much of the available literature, argues that this managerial style is autocratic, impulsive, egocentric and essentially unpredictable. Forward planning is limited and relations with employees are highly particularistic.

Of course, we must beware of over-generalisation here. There is no single entrepreneurial or owner-manager type but rather, as research has indicated (for example, Stanworth and Curran, 1973 and 1976), a range of entrepreneurial identities which result from a subtle interaction between type of economic activity, period of establishment of the enterprise, level of success and whether the small firm executives are first

13

generation entrepreneurs or those who have inherited ownership.   But
Kets de Vries has drawn the central contrast between the informal,
particularistic managerial style of small enterprise and the formal,
bureaucratic administration of the typical large enterprise.

One of the most interesting developments since the Bolton inquiry has
been the growth of small business pressure groups. The Committee
remarked on the ineffectiveness of small business pressure groups
(Bolton Report, 1971: 93) and the list of individuals and organisations
who made representations to the Committee (Bolton Committee, 1971:
Appendix IV) shows a notable absence of such groups. All this has now
changed and Britain's small business stratum is becoming a formidable
political influence.

This change has been discussed by McHugh (1979) who argues that this
increasing representation has taken two main forms. First, an increase
in the activities on behalf of the small businessman by bodies such as
the CBI who claim to speak for industry as a whole. The CBI has always
had an interest in the small firm but the increase in independent associations claiming to be exclusively concerned with small businessmans'
interests, has apparently stimulated the CBI to greater action. Second,
there has been a very public emergence of associations such as the
National Federation of Self-Employed and Small Businesses, established
in 1974 and which claimed a membership of 30,000 within its first six
months. Other similar bodies are the Association of Independent
Businesses, the Alliance of Small Firms and Self Employed People, the
Union of Independent Companies, and the Forum of Private Business.

The lobbying tactics of these groups have often been crude and blat-
antly self-seeking but they have won concessions from governments in
favour of the small business and made politicians of all parties much
more positive towards the smaller business. For instance, the present
Government increased the length of time before an employee could claim
unfair dismissal from six months to one year and the Employment Act of
1980 provided that for firms with twenty or fewer employees, the period
would be two years (Westrip, 1980).   Similar successes were achieved
in the 1980 and 1981 budgets which followed favourable treatment from
the previous Labour Government such as the abolition of capital transfer
tax on businesses transferred within a family.

14

Serious research on small business pressure groups has been limited but McHugh's analysis makes several key points. First, it is clear that, for a variety of reasons, there is an inherent tendency for such groups to fragment. Small business owner-managers are a highly hetero-geneous grouping with very differing interests, making it difficult for any single pressure group to effectively act on behalf of the small businessman and the self-employed.

Second, the representativeness of small business pressure groups may be questioned. Despite their successes, they have only recruited a relatively small proportion of their massive potential membership. The National Federation of the Self-Employed's own 1977 sample study of 7,500 members showed that the largest single grouping within their ranks were farmers (McHugh, 1978: 66). As the Federation's data also showed, there was a considerable membership wastage and a lot of recruiting effort was required simply to maintain their existing membership. As other studies have shown (Scase and Goffee, 1980) the small business owner-manager is very often a 'non joiner' - his commitment to the value of independence frequently precludes collective behaviour. More-over, where the enterprise has become a consuming life interest there may be little time or desire for outside activities.

Third, McHugh also shows that many of the leaders of small business pressure groups as well as many of the activists, have wider interests than the simple representation of the small business owner. These wider interests are often highly ideological and are indicated by the close association between the leaders of small business pressure groups and groups such as the National Association for Freedom (now the Freedom Association). Whether the majority of small business owner-managers are strongly committed to such ideologies is open to question. They may be broadly sympathetic but whether they are central to the practical con-cerns of running their enterprise is another matter.

Moreover, as Bechhofer and Elliott (1981) point out, the claim to speak on behalf of 'little capitalists' has been made increasingly by voices other than the small business pressure group thereby providing competition for the latter. For instance, several big companies have become economic and political sponsors for the small enterprise (as the activities of LEntA show, for example). The Conservative Party is attempting to recapture the support of the small enterprise owner with its own Small Business Bureau (established 1976) and the other main parties claim to favour the small enterprise as much as the present Government.

These wider political and ideological changes add up to what Bechhofer and Elliott call 'the defence of a moral economy' (1981: 190–91) through the emergence of a revived ideology of the new right in which the small business is the embodiment of the principles of independence, thrift, straight dealing, ingenuity and hard work. This ideology re-moralises capitalism, halting the slide into the practices and structures which have been labelled 'the unacceptable face of capitalism'. It seeks the return to a small scale, competitive business order where multi-nationals and the domination of the big corporation would somehow vanish. All told, these political and ideological shifts provide the most favourable ideological climate for the small business that has existed for decades in Britain.

THE SMALL FIRM EMPLOYEE: SOCIAL RELATIONS AND LABOUR MARKETS

The small firm employee was analysed in the Bolton Report entirely through the eyes of his or her employer. Because the small firm provided such a congenial work environment, employees were apparently willing to accept around 20 per cent less wages (Bolton Report, 1971: 21) and fewer fringe benefits. Conflict levels were also declared to be minimal (Bolton Report, 1971: 19). Other research (Ingham, 1970) reinforced this characterisation by introducing the notion of the self-selecting small firm worker whose main concern was with the intrinsic job satisfaction most likely to be found in the small firm.

Gradually, however, over the last decade this view of the small firm employee has been substantially modified and a more refined and detailed characterisation established. It is also one which, like the view of the small firm employer examined in the previous section, has started to take account of the links between the small enterprise and the wider society. This more recent and more complex view has several aspects. First, there is the 'meaning' of working in the small enterprise for the worker. Second, there are the findings concerning social relations in the small enterprise and especially those between employee and owner-manager. Thirdly, there are the links between employment experiences

16

and membership of the wider community and society.

The meanings associated with small firm employment are a great deal more complex than were supposed in 1971. For instance, studies of occupational placement patterns among manual workers show that job seeking is usually carried out haphazardly with little systematic knowledge: similar attitudes and behaviour have been found among small firm workers (Curran and Stanworth, 1979b). Small firm workers are more intrinsically minded than large firm workers but this appears to be much more related to life cycle position and labour market dynamics than to the enterprise. Small firm workers tend to be younger and are less likely to be married due to labour market influences and employer decisions. When such differences are controlled for, there appears little difference in levels of intrinsic mindedness among workers for a given industry, regardless of size of enterprise.

Job satisfaction among small firm workers also appears to be at odds with the Bolton Report views. The most recent study (Curran and Stanworth, 1981) suggests that, once age and marital state are controlled for, differences are small in relation to size of enterprise and that, indeed, type of industry is much more important than size of enterprise. The influence of type of industry may actually be so great as to reverse the expected small firm-intrinsic satisfaction relationship.

The comparison of material reward levels in small and large firms has turned out to be even more difficult than the Bolton Report recognised. Differences in skill levels, experience, worker reliability, job titles, job content, etc. are considerable even between firms of similar size in the same industry. An association has been noted between low pay and small enterprise employment but the exact nature of the relationship is unclear (Pond, 1979). Workers' views, however, do not support the notion that intrinsic satisfaction compensates for lower material rewards. In the survey noted above, although two out of three small firm workers believed their firm paid as well or better than any other firm they could work for (compared to 76 per cent of the large firm workers) the majority also believed that the firm could and should pay more. The findings that small firms offered fewer fringe benefits - especially as of right - was confirmed.

In research on social relations in the small enterprise, the most significant theoretical contribution to analysis has been that of Newby (1975 and 1977). This provides a subtle interpretation of small firm worker/owner-manager relations. The core of this interpretation is the insight that the major problem for the owner-manager is the attempt to maintain an inherently contradictory relationship with subordinates involving both differentiation and identification.

Differentiation involves the successful establishment and maintenance of superior-subordinate relations conforming to the acceptable organisational form of the enterprise in our culture - a hierarchical, market constrained enterprise whose performance is ultimately measured in terms of profit. Identification requires a moral involvement in the enterprise by the employee and particularistic relations between employee and owner-manager. These are characteristic of the managerial style of the small firm owner-manager as well as an outcome of the face to face relations of this form of enterprise.

Such relations are inherently contradictory because the logic of the free enterprise order dictates that the overriding constraint on the enterprise will be impersonal, cash nexus, profit and loss considerations: personal relations must always ultimately be subordinated to these. Yet small business owner ideologies stress the close personal relations based on an assumption of a harmony of interests between employer and employee. A good deal of the success of everyday social and economic relations in the enterprise will depend upon the goodwill generated between employer and employees. The vulnerability of the small business to the ups and downs of the market is a continuous, unpredictable reminder of these contradictions for all those involved.

A recent study by the Policy Studies Institute for the Manpower Services Commission (Daniel, 1981) reported that workers in small firms are more likely than others to lose their jobs. Forty-one per cent of their unemployed sample last worked for establishments employing less than twenty five people. This is, of course, no less than might be expected of workers employed in secondary sectors of the economy which are more vulnerable to the forces of recession and change than larger firms.

Attitudinal data from small firm studies reflect the above contradictions clearly. As the Bolton Report and its research reports (see

18

especially Golby and Johns, 1971: 40-44) implicitly revealed, small firm owner-managers have divergent views on their relations with their employees. On the one hand, they reported close, friendly and harmonious relations with 'their' workers but, on the other hand, they complained that they were increasingly unable to recruit and retain the kind of workers they sought because of the pernicious effects of modern society which had 'destroyed the will to work' and allowed the ordinary worker to dictate terms to the employer.

For their part, small firm employees find their firm a friendly place in which to work - friendlier than they believe a large firm would be (Ingham, 1970; Batstone, 1975; Curran and Stanworth, 1979a). But some researchers have also reported that this view can go hand in hand with reservations about the strength of the relationship with their employer and the extent to which it transcended the basic cash nexus connection (Curran and Stanworth, 1979a). In other words, the contradictory elements in the small firm employment relationship are recognised on this side of the fence also.

The third area of research - that concerning links between working in the small enterprise and membership of the wider social, economic and political order - has several facets. One of the most interesting which has developed in the 1970s is the notion of the segmented labour market (Bosanquet and Doeringer, 1973; Stolzenberg, 1978; Norris, 1978; Kreckel, 1980; Lawson, 1981).

A major distinction has been drawn between primary and secondary labour markets. Primary labour markets consist of mainly large firms who recruit the cream of the labour market - the well trained, well qualified, experienced and reliable personnel - by offering them a combination of good wages, promotion opportunities and fringe benefits. Secondary labour markets, on the other hand, consist of marginal firms recruiting marginal workers. The workers will be less well qualified and experienced, more likely to have an unstable work record, to be younger, to be immigrant workers or women or those without a trade union card.

Labour market analysis has a key bearing on the job creation potential of the small firm. A much cited study in relation to this aspect of the small firm is that of Birch (1979) which has widely (and mistakenly) been reported as showing that small firms in the United States created

19

over two-thirds of all new jobs, in the period 1969-76. However, Fothergill and Gudgin (1979) reporting the findings from a British study of job generation, found that although small firms were a rather better bet for employment growth than large firms, large firms create a large number of new jobs also. Put another way, while small firms may create more new jobs per unit of investment, they will only create a small percentage of all new jobs because large firms play a more substantial role in the economy as a whole (CBI, 1980: 34-39; Bannock, 1981: 97).

A further aspect of the worker/wider society relationship concerns the community location of the enterprise. Batstone (1975) argued that community was the crucial determinant of worker-management relations in small firms in semi-traditional Banbury. The 'ethos of small town capitalism' was the source of the close relations and shared views of his small firm workers and employers. Norris (1978) has incorporated this into an analysis of the broader, structural conditions required for the maintenance of paternalistic capitalism. Converseley, the absence of community factors favourable to close worker-employer relations have been shown to be associated with more distant relations (Curran and Stanworth, 1979a). Nationally, the growth of the welfare state, the emergence of a national culture through access to the mass media and particularly television, the increased emphasis on material consumption as the key to individual happiness and the decline of the close-knit local community through mobility and urban redevelopment, have all been factors undermining paternalistic capitalism.

Interest has also developed in small firm employee's political attitudes and behaviour, an interest which parallels the interest in the ideology and politics of small firm owner-managers. At the beginning of the 1970s, the accepted view was that the small firm worker was a 'working class deferential' who viewed society as a natural social order governed by those born to authority. The deferential might be near the bottom of this order but that was as things should be. He accepted a lowly position in return for the psychological rewards and security of belonging to a fixed, natural order and the opportunities for association with high status superiors. Such workers had few contacts with other members of the working class, were unlikely to join trade unions and were likely to vote Conservative (Lockwood, 1966;

Parkin, 1972).

Ingham (1969) argued that the small firm environment had an independent effect on political attitudes but his findings on voting behaviour were not entirely consistent with the idea of a small firm worker as a natural Conservative Party supporter. In a study of political attitudes and voting behaviour covering three of the General Elections of the 1970s, Curran (1980) found that there was little evidence for small firm workers having a deferential working class world view and that politically they were not strong Conservative supporters. Rather, they were distinguished by the volatility of their political allegiances and a propensity not to vote at all as compared to large firm workers. Like their employers, they were non-joiners, taking little part in voluntary associations of any kind as compared to the large firm workers in the study (Curran, 1981).

THE SMALL FIRM IN THE 1980s: AN AGENDA FOR RESEARCH

The research picture of the small enterprise in Britain that has emerged in the 1970s covers a wide range of aspects of the small firm and its functioning and is now solidly impressive compared to that available to the Bolton Committee.

The Bolton Report was modestly confident about the future of the small firm in Britain. While recognising that the small enterprise was in a state of long term decline, it also noted that such a decline was not in itself proof of any fundamental weakness in the small firm sector. No rational, research-based estimate of the optimum size distribution of firms in a modern economy was available (and neither is it in 1981). The small enterprise was a viable form of economic unit because in many areas it was economically and organisationally superior to the larger enterprise. It also performed a 'seed bed' function for the economy in the necessary process of economic regeneration which goes on all the time in a vital economy.

Subsequently, others such as Bannock (1976) felt the Committee had been too optimistic but the view from 1981 might be that the Committee was broadly correct in its estimates. Overall, the future for small firms seems at least as assured in 1981 as it did in 1971. One tendency which seems difficult to reverse is the temptation to talk of

21

'the small firm' as if small firms were a homogenous category. In
fact, research in the 1970s has established very clearly just how
erroneous this verbal convenience really is. We propose that small
firm researchers seek to systematically explore the specific influences
of industrial sub-cultures and community on the small enterprise. This
is not simply a matter of establishing variations in the socio-economic
form of enterprise but of establishing how size aspects subtly interact
with industrial and environmental influences. Particularly important
is to break out of the manufacturing sector, in which most research is
now concentrated, into other economic sectors especially white collar
industries, the service and new information sectors of the economy.

To this proposal we would add a plea for more research into 'uncon-
ventional' small enterprises such as franchising, those which form the
black economy and producer co-operatives. Some of these, such as black
economy entrepreneurs, will call for imaginative research designs but a
good deal of ingenuity has already been expended in constructing ways of
studying illegitimate economic behaviour (see, for example, Bryant,
1974). That an enterprise is illegitimate or illegal makes it no less
worthy of research or less important for the economy.

A further proposal is an example of research being initiated in areas
parallel to those already researched. A good deal is known about entrepreneurial and managerial ideologies in the small enterprise but we
know a good deal less about day to day managerial behaviour after the
initial period of setting up the enterprise. We know from other sources
(for example, Fishbein and Ajzen, 1975) that we cannot equate either
ideological declarations or public statements of practice with actual
behaviour. Yet a good deal of small business teaching and the prescrip-
tive literature on managing the small firm is based on very little well-
founded knowledge of the day to day functioning of the small firm.

Research on the small firm employee increased greatly in the 1970s but
the emphasis has been on the male shop floor worker and to a lesser
extent on supervisors. What is now required is more research on women
workers - assumed to be over-represented in the secondary labour market
by segmented labour market theorists - and on the employment of
specialist white collar employees. The small firm is sometimes said to
be unattractive to well qualified specialists such as engineers but
small firms have an effective record in research and development and

innovation. This apparent inconsistency suggests that small firms have ways of coping with their requirements for highly qualified workers and a fuller explanation of how this occurs might have considerable implications for understanding the small firm generally. Finally, more attention should be given to industrial relations in the small enterprise.

Proposals for research should also take into account anticipated developments. Too often researchers have only begun to take an interest in developments in the small firm sector some time after they have become well established. One development requiring immediate research attention is Enterprise Zones. For example, it has been argued that Enterprise Zones will produce no net increase in the number of small firms since Enterprise Zone firms, using their Zone advantages, will simply 'crowd out' other small firms in the immediate surrounding area.

Another hypothesis might be that the independence of thinking, the dislike of bureaucracy and official regulations, will discourage entre-preneurs from establishing in the Zones. This argument is sometimes reinforced by pointing out that the tax advantages - the primary incent-ive offered by the Zones - may not be very important in the formative period of the enterprise especially if, as seems to be happening, rising rents within the Zone discount tax advantages. Such a study might also inform our scanty knowledge of owner-manager/government relations more generally.

These sample proposals for research into the small firm in the 1980s are simply meant to make our final point. Research in the small firm in the 1980s will be as stimulating and exciting as it has been in the 1970s and, we believe, just as productive. The problem may be, as it became increasingly in the 1970s, that disseminating findings to teach-ers and policy makers (particularly the latter) does not always occur as fast as it should. The increasing sophistication of theorising and research designs may also raise communication problems. Generalisations may too easily be disseminated which distort the actual findings or even misrepresent them. Compared to 1971, we have a strong base from which to launch our research endeavours of the next decade and if we can achieve as much over the next decade as over the last, both policy makers and small businessmen will benefit and, indirectly, so will our whole society.

REFERENCES

Agarwal, N.C., 'On the Interchangeability of Size Measures', *Academy of Management Journal*, Vol.22, No.2, 1979.

Bannock, G., *The Smaller Business in Britain and Germany*, London, Wildwood House, 1976.

Bannock, G., *The Economics of Small Firms, Return from the Wilderness*, Oxford, Blackwell, 1981.

Batstone, E.V., *Aspects of Stratification in a Community Context: A Study of Class Attitudes and the 'Size Effect'*, PhD thesis, University of Wales, 1969.

Batstone, E.V., 'Deference and the Ethos of Small Town Capitalism' in Bulmer, M., (ed.) *Working-Class Images of Society*, London, Routledge and Kegan Paul, 1975.

Bechhofer, F., Elliott, B., Rushforth, M. and Bland, R., 'The Petits Bourgeois in the Class Structure, the case of the Small Shopkeepers' in Parkin, F. (ed.) *The Social Analysis of Class Structure*, London, Tavistock, 1974.

Bechhofer, F. and Elliott, B. 'Persistence and Change: the Petite Bourgeois in Industrial Society', *European Journal of Sociology*, Vol.XVII, 1976.

Bechhofer, F. and Elliott, B. (eds.) *The Petite Bourgeoisie, Comparative Studies of the Uneasy Stratum*, London, Macmillan, 1981.

Belbin, R.M., 'Launching New Enterprises, Some Fresh Initiatives for Tackling Unemployment', *Department of Employment Gazette*, Vol.88, No.4, 1980.

Bell, D., *The Coming of Post-Industrial Society*, London, Heinemann, 1974.

Birch, D., 'The Job Generation Process' M.I.T. Programme on Neighbourhood and Regional Change, Cambridge, Mass., MIT, 1979.

Bosanquet, N. and Doeringer, P.B., 'Is There a Dual Labour Market in Britain?', *Economic Journal*, Vol.83, 1973.

Boswell, J., *The Rise and Decline of Small Firms*, London, Allen and Unwin, 1973.

Brewers' Society (The), *Beer Facts 1981*.

Bryant, C.D., (ed.) *Deviant Behaviour, Occupational and Organisational Bases*, Chicago, Rand McNally, 1974.

CBI, *Smaller Firms in the Economy*, London, 1980.

Collins, O.F., Moore, D.G., with Unwalla, D.B., *The Enterprising Man*, East Lancing, Michigan State University Press, 1964.

Curran, J., 'The Political World of the Small Firm Worker', *Sociological Review*, Vol.28, No.1, February 1980.

Curran, J., 'Class Imagery, Work Environment and Community: Some Further Findings and a Brief Comment', *British Journal of Sociology*, Vol.XXXII, No.1, March 1981.

Curran, J. and Stanworth, J., 'Worker Involvement and Social Relations in the Small Firm', *Sociological Review*, Vol.27, No.2, May 1979a.

Curran J. and Stanworth, J., 'Self-Selection and the Small Firm Worker
- A Critique and an Alternative View', *Sociology*, Vol.13, No.3,
September 1979b.

Curran, J. and Stanworth, J., 'A New Look at Job Satisfaction in the
Small Firm', *Human Relations*, Vol.34, No.5, May 1981.

Daniel, W.W., *The Unemployed Flow, Stage I Interim Report*, London,
Policy Studies Institute, 1981.

Feige, E.L., 'The U.K.'s Unobserved Economy: A Preliminary Assessment',
Journal of Economic Affairs, July 1981.

*Financing of Small Firms (The), Interim Report of the Committee to
Review the Functioning of Financial Institutions*, Cmnd. 7503, London,
HMSO, 1979 (The Wilson Report).

Fishbein, M. and Ajzen, I., *Beliefs, Attitudes, Interaction and
Behaviour; An Introduction to Theory and Research*, Reading, Mass.,
Addison-Wesley, 1975.

Fothergill, S. and Gudgin, G., *The Job Generation Process in Britain*,
London, Centre for Environmental Studies, 1979.

Galbraith, J.K., *The New Industrial State*, Harmondworth, Penguin, 1969.

Gershuny, J., *After Industrial Society? The Emerging Self-Service
Economy*, London, Macmillan, 1978.

Gershuny, J. and Pahl, R.E., 'Britain in the Decade of the Three
Economies', *New Society*, 9 January 1980.

Golby, C.W. and Johns, G., *Attitude and Motivation, Committee of Inquiry
on Small Firms*, Research Report No.7, London, HMSO, 1971.

Goldthorpe, J.H. with Llewellyn, C. and Payne, C., *Social Mobility and
Class Structure in Modern Britain*, Oxford, Clarendon Press, 1980.

Gupta, N., 'Some Alternative Definitions of Size', *Academy of Management Journal*, Vol.23, No.4, 1980.

Ingham, G.K., 'Plant Size, Political Attitudes and Behaviour',
Sociological Review, Vol.17, November 1969.

Ingham, G.K., *Size of Industrial Organisation and Worker Behaviour*,
Cambridge University Press, 1970.

Institute of Petroleum (The), *Petroleum Retail Outlet Survey*, 1980.

Jones, D.C., 'Producer Co-operatives in Industrialised Western Economies',
British Journal of Industrial Relations, Vol.XVIII, No.2, July 1980.

Kets De Vries, M.F.R., 'The Entrepreneurial Personality: a Person at
the Crossroads', *Journal of Management Studies*, Vol.14, No.1,
January 1977.

Kimberley, J.R., 'Organisational Size and the Structuralist Perspective:
A Review, Critique and Proposal', *Administrative Science Quarterly*,
Vol.21, December 1976.

Kreckel, R., 'Unequal Opportunity Structure and Labour Market
Segmentation', *Sociology*, Vol.14, No.4, 1980.

Lawson, T., 'Paternalism and Labour Market Segmentation Theory' in
Watkinson, F. (ed.) *Essays in the Dynamics of Labour Markets*,
forthcoming.

Liles, P.R., 'Who are the Entrepreneurs', *MSU Business Topics*, Winter 1974.

Lockwood, D., 'Sources of Variation in Working Class Images of Society', *Sociological Review*, No.14, No.3, November 1966.

Mayer, K.B. and Goldstein, S., *The First Two Years: Problems of Small Firm Growth and Survival*, Washington, Small Business Administration, 1961.

McClelland, D.C., *The Achieving Society*, New York, Van Nostrand, 1961.

McHugh, J., 'The Self-Employed and the Small Independent Entrepreneur', in King, R. and Nugent, N. (eds.) *Respectable Rebels, Middle Class Campaigns in the 1970s*, London, Hodder and Stoughton, 1979.

Motor Agents' Association, figures supplied by Neal Marshall, MAA Economist, Legal and Commercial Department, 1981.

Newby, H., 'The Deferential Dialectic', *Comparative Studies in Society and History*, Vol.17, No.2, 1975.

Newby, H., 'Paternalism and Capitalism' in Scase, R. (ed.) *Industrial Society: Class, Cleavage and Control*, London, Allen and Unwin, 1977.

Newby, H., Bell, C., Rose, D. and Saunders, P., *Property, Paternalism and Power*, London, Hutchinson, 1978.

Norris, G.M. 'Industrial Paternalistic Capitalism and Local Labour Markets', *Sociology*, Vol.12, No.3, 1978.

Oakshott, R., *The Case for Worker Co-operatives*, London, Routledge and Kegan Paul, 1978.

Parkin, F., *Class Inequality and Political Order: Social Stratification in Capitalist and Communist Societies*, London, Paladin, 1972.

Pond, C., 'Small Change, Small Firms, Labour Law and Low Pay', *Low Pay Unit Bulletin*, No.29, October 1979.

Pugh, D.S., and Hickson, D.J., *Organisational Structure in its Context: The Aston Programme I*, London, Saxon House, 1976.

Pugh, D.S. and Hinings, C.R. (eds.) *Organisational Structures: Extensions and Replications, the Aston Programme II*, Farnborough, Saxon House, 1976.

Scase, R. and Goffee, R., *The Real World of the Small Business Owner*, London, Croom Helm, 1980.

Small Firms - Report of the Committee of Inquiry on Small Firms, London, Cmnd. 4811, HMSO, 1971 (The Bolton Report).

Stanworth, J. and Curran, J., *Management Motivation in the Smaller Business*, Epping, Gower Press, 1973.

Stanworth, J. and Curran, J., 'Growth and the Small Firm - an Alternative View', *Journal of Management Studies*, Vol.13, No.2, May 1976.

Stolzenberg, R.M., 'Bringing the Boss Back In: Employer Size, Employee Schooling and Socio-economic Achievement', *American Sociological Review*, Vol.43, 1978.

Thornley, J., *Workers Co-operatives: Jobs and Dreams*, London, Martin Robertson, 1981.

Westrip, A., 'A Study of Research into the Effects of Employment
Legislation on Small Firms' in Watkins, D., Stanworth, J. and
Westrip, A. (eds.) *Stimulating Small Firms*, London, Gower Press,
forthcoming.

NOTE

The most comprehensive recent bibliography on the small business is:
P. Dowell (ed.) *The London Business School Small Business Bibliography*,
London Graduate School of Business Studies, 1980 plus *First and
Second Supplements*, 1981.

II FINANCE AND TAXATION

The Banks and Bolton Ten Years On
FRANK GREENHOW

Bolton came at the end of an era. An era in which 'bigness' was encouraged and in which 'big was beautiful'. Official thinking and official policy was geared towards creating large enterprises and many of
the major corporate groupings which we have today came about as the
result of the work of the Industrial Reorganisation Corporation (IRC).
Even the mergers which brought into being the banks that we have today
occurred at the end of the 1960s.

However, by the end of the 1960s changes were taking place. Pendul-
ums swing and eventually they begin their return tracks. The Bolton
Committee was appointed while the pendulum was still at the top of its
arc. If the President of the Board of Trade (as the office was then
called) had delayed appointing a Committee for say, twelve or eighteen
months, it is possible that the Bolton Report would never have been
published.

Up until the end of the 1960s small firms were at a disadvantage compared with larger firms when competing for funds. This very fact was
one of the major reasons why the Committee was established. The qualitative and quantitative controls which had been imposed on bank lending
since the war meant that, when it came to allocating scarce resources,
the larger established and therefore proven and more creditworthy enterprises were given first consideration for the available funds and newer,
smaller and, almost by definition, more risky enterprises were naturally
at the bottom of the pile. There was little point in the banks, for
example, competing in the market for funds if the effect of controls
meant that they were unable to on-lend them.

By the beginning of the 1970s, however, this situation had changed.
Two months before the publication of Bolton, the old monetary system had
been swept away and in September 1971 Competition and Credit Control

(CCC) was introduced.   This did away with rationing of funds and credit ceilings and allowed funds to be allocated on the lines of the price mechanism.   The old barriers preventing funds reaching small businesses had been breached and since that time the flow of funds and the expansion of services to small businesses have known few bounds.

The main benefits to emerge from Bolton were that for the first time since the MacMillan Report of 1931, the small business sector was given credit for the vital part it plays in the national economy.   A review of the small business sector was long overdue and the facts and figures compiled for the report, together with the wealth of supporting evidence submitted by over 400 associations and individual firms, provided a tremendous input to economic knowledge of small businesses.   Of the recommendations made by the Committee, outstanding among those implemented was the establishment of the Small Firms Division of the Department of Trade and Industry and the setting up of the Small Firms Advisory Bureau which nowadays plays such an important role.   (other recommendations Bolton Report: 345 et seq.)

The Wilson Committee to review the functioning of Financial Institutions was appointed in January 1977 and, not to put too fine a point on it, came about as a result of political pressures to nationalise parts of the banking and other sectors of the financial system.   As a by-product of the general mass of evidence submitted the special place occupied by small firms was reviewed separately.   In view of the fact that small businesses account for about 90 to 95 per cent of all firms it is not surprising that their needs and requirements become apparent.

The ever present problems and difficulties of small firms were again aired and the Committee made its recommendations against the backdrop that there were infinitely more financial avenues open to large firms than small firms, especially the procurement of longer term equity and venture capital.   The main recommendations included a loan guarantee scheme, an English Development Agency and an expansion of the Over the Counter Market (OMC).

THE EFFECTS OF COMPETITION AND CREDIT CONTROL

Even so long after the introduction of Competition and Credit Control in September 1971, it is very difficult to distinguish between its direct effects and other factors which were the cause of other major changes in the course of the economy. In introducing Competition and Credit Control the then Governor of the Bank of England said that the basis of the proposals was to introduce a system under which the allocation of credit was primarily determined by its cost. Just as the abandonment by the clearing banks of their interest rate agreements and automatic links with Bank Rate were essential requisites for a competitive market so too were the removal of 'ceiling' and qualitative controls on bank lending, for these had inhibited interest rate competition for more than a decade. There had been no point in banks competing for deposits so long as they were actively prevented from making profitable use of them.

It is not intended here to review in depth the mechanics of the new arrangements nor the subsequent changes in the international monetary scene which forced changes upon the UK's domestic economic front. Suffice it to say that these resulted at various times in frequent qualitative directives to the banks, a ceiling on interest payable upon seven-day deposits of under £10,000, and the introduction of the supplementary deposit scheme. Nevertheless, through it all the original fabric of CCC remained more or less intact.

Whilst there were problems with Credit Control, so far as competition is concerned it was certainly successful - even too successful for the authorities clearly underestimated the pent-up demand for credit and the mobility of short term funds in response to small interest rate differentials. It can now be seen that the expansion in lending in 1972-73 was far too rapid and that problems of inflation can in some measure be attributed to its excessive growth. The banks can hardly be criticised for responding to the freedom to compete in the way the authorities intended them to by taking every advantage of the opportunities available and thus contributing to the very rapid growth of the economy.

Competition and Credit Control is often said to have been a significant factor in diverting resources from essential industries, such as manufacturing and exports, to non-priority users such as the property and financial sectors, and to the personal sector. In fact, whilst there were substantial increases in lending to the latter sectors, advances to manufacturing industry increased even more and it was never suggested that these essential industries suffered from lack of needed funds.

The banking system, and particularly the clearing banks, derived considerable benefits from the introduction of Competition and Credit Control. Increased deposits and volume of lending coupled with higher interest rates led to higher profits which, after taxation, the banks ploughed back to strengthen their capital bases thus enabling them to do even more. The clearing banks also rapidly expanded their international operations and came close to the top of the world league of international banks.

In the home market the freedom to compete led to product innovation by way of credit card operations, personal loans and home improvement loans, and many other services for the personal sector. More importantly, especially for small firms, the banks made great efforts to introduce comprehensive financial services and to innovate by creating new products. In NatWest, for example, the Business Development Loan was introduced in 1971 hard on the heels of Competition and Credit Control.

It is fair to conclude that, in spite of the drawbacks which arose in Credit Control, the freedom to compete produced advantages which overall considerably outweighed the deficiencies of Credit Control.

THE BANKS AND THE SMALL BUSINESS SECTOR TODAY

It has been shown how the introduction of Competition and Credit Control led to a new competitive spirit in banking which in turn produced new products. Nevertheless, the banks have continued to be the subject of much criticism regarding the role they play in industrial finance. Whilst much of this criticism came from the Press, more importantly, criticism has also been coming from educational and research establishments, small business advisers and their representative bodies, and small businessmen themselves.

Since both Bolton and Wilson fundamentally agreed that the present system was able to produce the funds needed, the emphasis of the criticism has now shifted towards the banks' alleged inflexibility towards the small business sector and their general unwillingness to accept a higher degree of risk. It must be stressed that banks have a duty to lend depositors money safely. In the fringe bank crisis it was seen all too clearly what may happen if this simple rule is not followed. Sir

Jeremy Morse (Chairman of Lloyds Bank and also of the Committee of
London Clearing Bankers) said recently at this year's Institute of
Bankers Cambridge Seminar, that there are limitations of prudence and
practicality which govern how far institutions that are large takers of
customers' short term balances can lend money at term or at high risk.

THE BANKS' SERVICES TO SMALL BUSINESS

In responding to the needs of small firms the Banks have developed a
range of services which, whilst being broadly similar, do have significant technical differences.

Overdrafts

The Clearing Banks' overdraft remains the most versatile and the most
popular form of borrowing for the small business.   Within the agreed
limits the advance can fluctuate freely in response to the needs of the
business.   It is a short term borrowing, designed to provide working
capital.   Interest is charged on a day-to-day basis and the overdraft
tends to be cheaper than other forms of finance.   Overdrafts are generally intended to cover short term borrowing needs such as financing
the purchase of stock and work in progress where sale of the finished
product generates funds to repay the borrowing.

It became of concern to the Banks that a number of these short term
borrowings tended to develop a hard core primarily because they had been
used to finance rather longer term purchases of plant and machinery.
This type of investment should be financed through permanent or longer
term funds where the commitment may be spread evenly over a number of
years.   If small firms had ready access to the Stock Market or to
private sources of equity and loan capital, the problem might not have
occurred. As things are, banks have for some time understood the need
to complement the overdraft facility with other forms of loan finance.

Special Lending Schemes

In recent years term loans have formed an increasing proportion of the
clearing banks' total lending to small firms.   These include conventional medium term loans and term lending schemes designed with the needs of

the small firm in mind. An important feature of some of these schemes is the option that small businesses now enjoy to repay at a fixed rate of interest rather than a variable one. Even where the rate is variable, the monthly repayments often remain unchanged because movements in interest rates are accommodated by adjustments in the length of the repayment period.

These schemes are extremely popular, in contrast to the bank's equity finance packages which are only encountering modest demand. The principal schemes may be summarised as follows:

(a) Barclays Business Expansion Loans are available to finance capital investment for small/medium size companies with successful trade records and growth prospects. Up to £500,000 and up to 100 per cent of the asset cost may be borrowed. Interest rates may be fixed or floating and although security is normally required, it may be waived. Repayment periods are not expected to be longer than the life of the asset and capital repayment may be deferred for two years.

(b) Barclays Start-Up loans for new companies or companies with new products. Up to £50,000 over a period of five years. No capital repayments are required until five years have passed. The cost of the loan is expressed as a percentage of sales rather like a Royalty.

(c) Lloyds Asset Loans for between £5,000-£25,000 to finance up to 100 per cent of premises, vehicle and equipment costs. A fixed interest rate is charged and the advance is normally secured.

(d) Lloyds Enterprise Loan for up to £250,000 for development purposes. The interest is linked to the Bank's Base Rate and the advance is normally secured. Repayment 'rest periods' may be negotiated.

(e) Midland offers a long term loan scheme whereby amounts of £20,000-£50,000 may be repaid over periods of 10-20 years. Security is required but the borrower may opt for either a variable or a fixed rate of interest and a holiday on capital repayments of up to two years may be arranged. Venture loans of up to £250,000 over periods of 1-10 years are also available.

(f) NatWest provides fixed interest rate Business Development Loans of £2,000–£100,000 on a secured or unsecured basis repayable over periods of up to ten years.

In all cases the interest rates on unsecured loans will be slightly higher to take into account the risk element involved.

Loan Guarantee Scheme

In June 1981 the Loan Guarantee Scheme was launched under which the Government accepts 80 per cent of the risk and the Banks the remaining 20 per cent.

As already noted, this scheme formed one of the recommendations of the Wilson Report but the banks were initially sceptical about the need for such a scheme because they feared the bureaucratic process which might accompany it. However, once the details became clear, the banks have participated fully in the scheme as is evidenced by the take up rate of these loans.

The scheme was introduced as an experiment for three years with the Government setting aside £50m for the first year. Loans of up to £75,000 are granted for periods of between two and seven years. Interest rates are fixed by the participating banks and vary between 2 per cent and 3 per cent over base rate plus an arrangement fee. The Department of Industry charges a premium of 3 per cent of the guaranteed portion of the loan with the intention of making the scheme self-financing.

Applicants must be prepared to pledge all available assets used, or available for use, in the business as security for guaranteed loans, though this does not exclude from the Scheme cases where no assets are available. Finally, the proposition must be viable and one where the Bank could not lend without the benefit of the Government Guarantee.

Long Term Finance (up to 20 years)

The Clearing Banks do provide a limited range of long term finance to companies with undoubted potential for growth and a proven ability to provide an adequate return on the investment. They do not, however, see their primary function in this field. The Barclays Business Expansion Loan is sometimes granted up to this time scale.

The Clearing Banks themselves do not see the provision of Equity Finance
as part of their traditional range of services. The principal objection
to this type of activity is that it involves placing depositors' money
into areas of high risk.   Of late, however, there have been movements
in this direction through their Merchant Banking subsidiaries. It has
been shown elsewhere in this paper the economic scenario of the last
decade has prevented many small businesses from amassing equity from
retained profits or from private means. Access to the Stock Market is
also difficult. With this in mind equity finance has been made available for various situations, for example, to enable families to maintain
control over their firms and to create and preserve new and existing
firms.

All of the big 4 banks now have equity investment facilities.   The
Midland in fact has six wholly or jointly owned subsidiaries in the
Midland Bank Industrial Equity Holdings group of companies.   Individual
investments of up to £2m (occasionally more) are made.   The equity
participation is never more than 49 per cent, and the Bank does not seek
board room representation.

The Barclays Bank subsidiary Barclays Development Capital makes equity
investments of £100,000 or more to companies whose net worth is between
£250,000 and £10m.   As with the Midland the maximum equity involvement
is 49 per cent with a usual range of 10-30 per cent.

Lloyds Bank have recently created Pegasus Holdings Ltd through which
they will invest £100,000+ in companies with a sound trade record and
proven management.   The equity involvement will be between 10-33 per
cent.

National Westminster Bank follows a slightly different line insofar
as its Capital Loan Scheme involves the provision of fixed rate unsecured subordinated loans of up to £100,000.   These loans are for periods
of up to ten years and are coupled with an <u>option</u> to subscribe to up to
49 per cent of the company equity, though usually the option is for less
than 25 per cent.

Other Forms of Finance

Instalment credit and leasing are more often appropriate than overdrafts and loans for financing plant and equipment. All the banks now have subsidiary companies providing financing and leasing facilities. This type of financing is useful to customers who require to invest in new plant but do not wish to make the direct capital expenditure themselves.

Another type of facility available is factoring. Most of the Clearing Banks now have subsidiaries or associates specialising in a factoring service. To some degree it is a hybrid service performing four functions:

a) Bookkeeping and sales ledger administration, which includes the responsibility for despatching invoices and ensuring that they are paid.

b) Providing credit information regarding the standing of a person with whom a company is doing business.

c) In the case of non-recourse factoring agreements the factor guarantees payment on all approved sales.

d) Factors will advance up to 80 per cent of the value of invoices despatched. Interest is charged.

Firms are able to use this service if their turnover is above a certain level, e.g. £200,000, and invoices are over, say, £60 on average. It is a useful service for small firms because it avoids the need to maintain a sophisticated sales ledger. It can be of great assistance where sales are expanding rapidly as experience shows it often results in a speedier settlement of debts and greatly improves the cash flow.

Business Advisory Services

Two of the Clearing Banks currently operate a Business Advisory Service designed to aid the small businessman. These provide a consultancy service, free to customers, on such matters as costing, budgeting, cash-flow, forecasting and investment appraisal. Systems are suggested to deal with paper flow etc. The recommendations, which are confidential, suggest how the customer can save money, improve efficiency, or use further capital.

THE BANKS AND EDUCATION

The Bolton Report highlighted the fact that the small businessman was
not aware of the range of facilities available to him, their advantages
and disadvantages, nor how to present his case before the Bank Manager.
The crux of the matter was that he was not financially educated, nor
were the banks taking a positive attitude towards rectifying this short
coming. During the decade since the Report the Banks have realised the
extent to which this problem relates to the major internal problem of
educating their own managers to a level where they are aware of the
smaller firms difficulties.

Internal Education

Throughout the decade press opinion and adverse criticism have caused
the Banks to increase the amount of attention given to the Small Business Sector. All have tried, through the medium of internal training,
to educate their managers towards a more flexible approach.   The problems of quality outlined by Bolton still remain. Some human beings are
always going to be far more cautious in their approach than others.
Different personalities, fears of making mistakes, and all kinds of
human psychological factors will mean that this fact is difficult to
overcome. Nevertheless, efforts are being made through the medium of
local Regional and Area Conferences, Video Films and external courses.
This year, the Institute of Bankers is conducting a series of seminars/
meetings throughout the country for their own members on the subject of
small business. These meetings will be on an 'industry wide' basis and
attendance will range from management down to junior levels.

External Education

The emphasis on external education is taking place on two broad fronts.
Firstly, to let the small businessman know precisely what facilities
are available and secondly to show him how best to approach his Bank
Manager. The first aspect can be adequately covered by the range of
publicity material and brochures currently being produced for small
businesses. Needless to say there is a distinct marketing slant in all
publications which are designed to sell a Bank's services.   Some pub-

lications deal with specific services whilst others view matters over the whole range. Most banks also publish specific and very comprehensive guides to help businessmen in the export market.

Viewing the more general aspects of education, the activities of the Clearing Banks are widespread. They actively participate in the many courses run for small businessmen and women by discussing banking and finance with prospective entrepreneurs. The content of these talks cover the financial schemes available, both how to draw up propositions and other ways in which the banks can help both the new business and the established one.

As individuals a number of bank personnel do make themselves available as counsellors in local situations and through the local medium of the businessman's club or Chamber of Commerce. Whilst not being a particular activity of the banks, it is as a result of the increased awareness of bank staff of the need for involvement, that they have become familiar with the needs of small firms at the same time as showing them how to help their Bank Manager help them.

It is now becoming more frequent for Bankers to take part in local 'brains trust' and attend and talk at local business meetings. In certain instances Banks have arranged local seminars themselves in order to put the message across.

In April the National Westminster Bank began publishing a quarterly Small Business Digest. This contains articles on finance and banking in general and is aimed at bridging the information and communication gap. It is aimed at firms employing up to fifty people, though feedback indicates that it is widely read by people in companies with up to as many as 2,000 employees. It has a print run of nearly 400,000 copies and is distributed via trade, management and small business journals. More recently the Co-operative Bank has started a newsletter for small businesses.

It is perhaps relevant also to mention here the secondments which banks, in common with other major companies, make to enterprise agencies, advice centres and other similar ventures supporting the small business sector. Such secondments provide the receiving organisations with experience they could not usually afford to buy in and the secondees are exposed to a variety of problems which test their resourcefulness and

ingenuity to the full. The banks benefit from the feedback on the
small business scene, the broadened experience of those seconded upon
their return to banking and from being seen to support the communities
in which they operate. In some instances banks, in common with other
socially responsible companies, provide financial grants to these organisations to help meet formation expenses and/or running costs.

Most of the activities outlined in this section have been gradually
increasing during the past few years and have been executed without a
great deal of publicity. The degree of involvement of the Banks and
their staff is probably greater than most people are aware.

CONCLUSIONS

In the ten years since Bolton reported very significant and fundamental
changes have taken place. Broadly speaking these are the introduction
of Competition in 1971 and the change in attitude towards the small
firm sector.

This sector is a very important one to the banks. In NatWest bank,
for example, the ratio of small businesses to large is around 10 to 1 -
without it the corporate sector in numerical terms would be negligible.
Moreover, it is a very large and healthy one in which about half of the
small business customers employ less than ten people. The situation is
much the same in all the major clearers. The banks, freed from the
restraints which had prevented them from competing, have developed a
wide range of services, and the Loan Guarantee Scheme appears to be an
important addition to that range.

The problem today is that there is a significant communications gap
between small businesses and the banks, and this is something to which
all the banks are addressing themselves through their social responsibility programmes, through in-house training and through the many
courses and seminars available to help the small business man or woman.

But if it was true at the time of Bolton and of Wilson that there was
no evidence that the small business sector lacked sources of finance it
must be truer than ever today when one looks at the multiplicity of
schemes available from the banks ten years on from Bolton.

ACKNOWLEDGEMENT

The author would like to acknowledge the help of Bill Hodgson of National Westminster Bank's Market Intelligence Department and Peter Jarvis in the preparation of this Paper.

Tax Anomalies and the Small Firm
JOE HORNER

The Bolton Committee emphasised that what is needed is a taxation policy
which will restore initiative, encourage entrepreneurial activity and
improve the liquidity position of small businesses. Thirteen specific
recommendations were made. Most of those recommendations have been
followed up in the succeeding ten years. Our gratitude is due to the
members of the Bolton Committee for presenting the case for these amend-
ments so persuasively.

Despite these improvements, there are still many anomalies and irrita-
tions in the tax system which detract from the value of the small
business sector to the economy as a whole. Many of these anomalies are
not limited to the small business sector but have a more serious effect
on this sector than on other sectors.

CAPITAL OR REVENUE

There are many occasions when expense needs to be incurred for the
maintenance or expansion of a business and there are alternative ways of
incurring the expense. In considering the costs of the alternative, the
trader has to bear in mind the taxation consequences of his decision and
it sometimes transpires that what is a less efficient approach on normal
commercial criteria may be the most economic approach after taking into
account the tax effects.

An example of this principle could be the case where a trader has a
storage building which is dilapidated and possibly even dangerous. The
building is essential for the business and some form of remedial action
must be taken. He obtains quotations from builders and property
repairers and discovers that it would be cheaper to knock down the building and rebuild it than to prop it up and make good all the defects in

it. The cost for knocking down and rebuilding might be, say, £15,000 and the cost for making good might be £20,000. Obviously, at first sight it may attract him to knock down and rebuild. However, the cost of improvements, alterations or replacements are not tax deductible expenses because they are of a capital nature and therefore to spend £15,000 the business will need a net outlay of £15,000. The alternative method of repair is classified as revenue expenditure and therefore is chargeable in calculating taxable profits of the business. If the effective tax rate of the business at the relevant time is 40 per cent the payment of £20,000 will reduce the tax bill by £8,000 and therefore the net cost to the business will be only £12,000. What appeared to be the more expensive approach is transformed by the tax allowance into the less expensive.

The example above is an over-simplification. By spending the money on a capital improvement, it is possible that the business may obtain a long term allowance on some future capital gain. The trader must therefore, in considering the comparative costs, try to anticipate whether a chargeable gain is likely to arise in the future; if so when; and what the future value of the tax allowance is in relation to the current value of the alternative allowance.

What should be a simple decision is converted by the tax system into a very difficult decision. In addition, the knowledge that the tax system can have this important effect on the net cost of a project means that the trader may always feel compelled to obtain expensive professional advice before doing something which should be simple and straightforward.

MACHINERY AND PLANT

It is not always a disadvantage for expenditure to be classed as capital expenditure rather than revenue expenditure. In particular, if the work on which expenditure is incurred comes within the meaning of 'machinery and plant' it can be more advantageous than a similar amount of expenditure which is classified as revenue expenditure.

If a business is conducted by a sole trader or a partnership the tax assessment for any year is not normally based on the profit for that year but on the profit for a 'basis period'. Some trading periods form the basis period for more than one tax year; most trading periods form the basis period for only one tax year; and some trading periods form the basis period for no tax years at all. Revenue expenditure which falls in a trading period which does not form a basis period for a tax assessment is really ineffective and obtains no tax relief whereas the same amount of expenditure which could be classified as capital expenditure on machinery and plant will obtain tax relief. On the other hand, if expenditure is in a period which forms a basis period for more than one tax year revenue expenditure might effectively enjoy tax relief twice over or more whilst capital expenditure on machinery and plant would only enjoy tax relief once.

The current rate of allowance which can be claimed for expenditure on machinery and plant is 100 per cent of the outlay at the time of outlay. However, it is not compulsory to claim the full amount. If a lesser amount is claimed the remaining expenditure can be claimed in other tax years. This flexibility can sometimes make the capital allowances more attractive than revenue expenditure.

If a business incurs losses in any trading period, there are provisions which allow it to set these losses against earlier or future profits or against other income. To the extent that losses are attributable to first year allowances, the choices of how the relief can be applied are wider so that once again this type of capital expenditure is more favourably treated than revenue expenditure.

'Machinery and plant' is not defined and there are often very great problems in knowing whether an item does fall within the meaning and therefore can enjoy tax relief or whether it is on the wrong side of the undefined line and therefore enjoys no relief. It is highly likely that many taxpayers fail to claim on items which could qualify because they or their inexperienced advisers are unaware of the principles involved.

INDUSTRIAL AND OTHER BUILDINGS

Capital allowances can be claimed on industrial buildings. The allowances are related to the cost of construction. As with machinery and plant, there are many borderline disputes on the question of whether a building falls within the definition or not.

Apart from the difficulties of deciding whether a particular building
is within the appropriate definition or not, another anomaly is in the
implicit belief that manufacturing and certain allied businesses are to
receive encouragement from the tax system whilst other businesses are
not deserving of such encouragement. A factory qualifies for relief
regardless of the fact that it might be making socially undesirable
products or that it is supplying an already over-supplied market whilst
another building such as a dental surgery, a shop or a play school in a
deprived area which undoubtedly performs a valuable service to the
community will receive nil encouragement.

Agricultural buildings and works and also newly constructed hotels
also enjoy capital allowances and a more recent innovation is the grant-
ing of allowances on commercial buildings in enterprise zones. Because
these zones have a geographical limit there can be anomalies between
the treatment of very similar businesses which are close together but
are on different sides of the physical boundary. These difficulties
can extend beyond the tax field.

It is quite likely that some traders or landlords who would be entitled to tax relief for industrial or other buildings if they understood the principles of the relief and had access to all the relevant
facts do not claim because of a failure of understanding or of information.

INCONSISTENCY OF INTERPRETATION

In the above matters and in many other aspects of taxation the wording
of the law is imprecise. Many High Court cases have been taken to try
to establish the meaning of certain words and phrases and it is custo-
mary for accountants and others to study past and current decisions with
a view to seeing how close the facts in a legal precedent are to the
facts relating to their clients. However, it is impossible for all
Inspectors to place the same interpretation on the same set of facts.
What is accepted without challenge in one tax office may be disputed in
another office. The cost, in time and money, of establishing the
correct interpretation is frequently prohibitive. Many accountants
will be familiar with the situation where they and their clients believe
that tax relief is available for a certain transaction, but the Tax

Inspector thinks otherwise and the accountant has reluctantly to advise his client that he must yield to the Tax Inspector's interpretation because the cost of proving the Inspector wrong would be more than the tax involved.

It is not a criticism of the personnel employed in the Inland Revenue to say that bad decisions are often made. (It would also be very wrong to imply that bad decisions are not also made from the other side of the fence.) Tax law has become so complicated that no one person can claim to be a master of it. Even where cases reach the High Courts, a case which is decided in one direction may be overturned by a higher court or there may be split decisions in the Court of Appeal or House of Lords. From this it is obvious that highly trained legal minds cannot agree on interpretations in many cases and therefore it would be unreasonable to assume that accountants and Tax Inspectors who have much more limited time in which to consider individual cases could invariably produce the right answer.

INLAND REVENUE INVESTIGATIONS

A very great difficulty which is receiving increasing comment is the attitude of the Inland Revenue when examining the accounts of small businesses. A Tax Inspector has a duty to satisfy himself that the accounts produced to him do show the true results of the trading of a business. If he feels that the accounts do not do this he must try to establish what the true trading profit is and in addition to this he must try to decide why a wrong figure has been produced.

There are penalties for making wrong declarations but the penalty will vary depending on whether there is a genuine misunderstanding; whether there is neglect; or whether there is wilful default or fraud. In most cases the Inland Revenue do not seek to apply the maximum penalty which the law permits. Having tried to satisfy himself regarding the degree of culpability of the tax payer, a Tax Inspector is empowered to make a compromise settlement accepting less than the full amount of penalty which could be enforced.

A Tax Inspector will have his own idea of how successful a business should be. In recent years the Inland Revenue have tried to collate information which will assist the Inspector. For instance they will study the accounts of a wide range of, say, restaurants and will form some idea of what gross profit margins can be expected and what various overheads might be. If the accounts produced for one business fall short of what the Inspector anticipates he is in a position effectively to put the onus on the tax payer to prove that his accounts are right. This can be very difficult particularly where large amounts of cash are handled. A person who is slightly unfortunate or not acquisitive enough in his business may therefore find that not only is he less well remunerated than other people, but that he is the object of Inland Revenue suspicions. An Income Tax investigation can be a very agonising, protracted, and expensive operation. Unless the tax payer keeps perfect business records he may find it very difficult to repel the Tax Inspector's charges. Most small traders will know that it is extremely difficult to keep records in perfect order. A person who is trying to do many aspects of the job at the same time will inevitably give his highest priority to satisfying his customers and his financial control and recording may leave something to be desired. A Tax Inspector has only to demonstrate that there is the scope for error or worse and he can very often then produce his own variation of what profit may have been earned and effectively challenge the tax payer to disprove it.

Whilst it is probable that most Inspectors use a great deal of discretion, tact and commonsense in pursuing their enquiries, it is also clear that others are over zealous and can cause great hardship to a business. Whilst it should not be suggested that such Inspectors are not sincere in their actions, it should be realised that an Inspector whose judgment is erratic does have the scales tilted very heavily in his favour and is in a position to perpetrate a grave injustice.

It is possible that the answer to this very difficult problem might lie in some system whereby a tax payer whose accounts or returns are challenged become entitled to make an early 'payment into Court'. If the results of a subsequent investigation should show that this payment was adequate to cover tax lost plus interest, the tax payer should then be able to recover the costs of further investigations. There are clearly difficulties in a proposal of this kind, but there is also the merit that it might curb the over-enthusiasm of the few Inspectors who at present cause costs and heartache out of all proportion to any offences committed or suspected.

TIMING

There are many features of the tax system where timing is too important. A simple example is that of a person who completes accounts to a date when his stockholding is at its highest. The system of stock relief now in force gives a reduction in an assessment dependent upon the amount of stock at one particular date in the year. A person who holds high stocks at that date has an advantage over another person who may hold a higher average level of stock throughout the year but whose level is not particularly high at the critical date.

There are many examples where a transaction will have a vastly different tax result if carried out a few days earlier or a few days later than the natural date which would occur if purely commercial criteria were applied. When a trader knows that timing is critical it will create uncertainty and expense.

VOLATILITY

Income Tax is an annual tax. A person who has nil income in one year and £30,000 in the following year will pay far more tax than another person who has income of £15,000 in each of those two years. The same point can be made at much lower levels.

The problem of volatility is much greater in some trades and professions than in others. Perhaps entertainers and sportsmen are the most extreme examples where a person can struggle for many years and then have a very lucrative period which may however be quite short. The prosperous period may again be followed by a very depressed period. To avoid the impact of the very high taxes which occur in the successful years, many people have taken up residence abroad. They are then sometimes criticised for being unpatriotic when perhaps they were escaping from a very unjust system rather than seeking to avoid the just application of a reasonable system. By failing to face up to this problem and trying to find a remedy the authorities have let the country be deprived of the earnings and the tax which could have been available under a fairer system.

There are a few provisions which do allow income to be spread over a period. These apply for artists and authors and to a smaller extent to

farmers, but there are many other areas where a person does not have
stability and job security and where the right to spread income for
tax purposes would go some way towards creating justice and equality.

TIME LIMITS

The law specifies time limits within which various elections and claims
must be made or within which action should be taken or avoided.   The
time limits are frequently too short for proper decisions to be made.
In particular there are two year limits for claiming or waiving capital
allowance claims; for making stock relief claims; and for deciding
how losses should be utilised. On the other hand some time limits are
absurdly generous. A person who is entitled to a higher personal allowance because he gets married has six years within which to make a claim
although there can be no difficulty whatsoever in establishing the facts
necessary to support the claim.

  One particularly frustrating time limit was the two year time limit
for claiming stock relief. The Government introduced a relief which
carried advantages and potential disadvantages. There was a two year
time limit within which to claim but it was very difficult for many
people to assess within that time limit whether the disadvantages outweighed the advantages. The Government then made significant changes
which took away or reduced the disadvantages but did not extend the
time limits. The result was that some cautious and well advised tax
payers failed to claim while others who had not appreciated the adverse
implications at the beginning did claim and then were protected from
their folly by later changes in the law.

MISTRUST OF GOVERNMENT

From many of the preceding paragraphs it is apparent that a tax payer
can suffer very heavily because of what are mere technicalities. If
compared with an equally successful tax payer whose income happens to
fall at different times or under different headings he may suffer excessive taxation. Tax Inspectors will frequently recognise that the
law they are applying is unjust, but they will point out that they have
no power to vary it. They will point apologetically to the dictum of a

High Court Judge that 'equity and income tax are strangers'. It is partially in response to this attitude (although one could not deny that it is also partially due to reluctance to accept a fair burden) that various 'tax avoidance' schemes were devised. These schemes sought to find technicalities which worked in favour of the tax payer and thereby to reduce the tax burden. For anybody seeking to take advantage of such a scheme there was always a risk that the technicalities were not quite as absurd as they had seemed and that the scheme did not work. On one occasion however there was a technicality of which advantage had been taken and the Government took steps to change the law retrospectively in order to withdraw the advantage. Whilst it is understandable that to many people in the media the issue of tax avoidance looks like a simple question of wealthy people trying to avoid paying their fair share towards the running of the country, it is regrettable that far too little publicity is given to the other side of the coin whereby the country itself inflicts an inequitable burden on some people - many of whom are not in fact conspicuously successful or wealthy.

One ironic feature of the Government's attack on tax avoidance is that the Government itself promoted tax reduction on a far greater scale than any other fiscal planners. It has been said that the old scheme of stock relief was devised by a financial illiterate. Certainly it was based on a most superficial understanding of the workings of industry and commerce. It reduced the tax burden of many businesses where there was a very good case for reducing the burden but it also significantly reduced the burden of other businesses where it would be much more difficult to claim that there was hardship. At the same time it denied relief to many people who were undoubtedly deserving of consideration and it had ripple effects throughout the economy which damaged other businesses. The overall effect was that tax was levied almost capriciously regardless of the success or merit of businesses and that the concept of a tax payer having a moral obligation to contribute a reasonable share was disastrously undermined.

UNPAID TAX COLLECTION

The small trader is an unpaid tax collector. VAT, PAYE and National Insurance are time consuming and frequently expensive to operate. The

businessman is in effect collecting tax from other people and acting as
the Agent of the Government. If he makes a mistake he can be held
responsible for the other person's tax and may not have the ability to
recover it.

It is partially because of this and partially because of other
employer/employee legislation which many employers regard as an unfair
burden that there have been moves towards the use of sub-contract labour
rather than full employees. The Government has been more concerned at
a possible loss of tax from this trend than about the underlying causes
and has therefore tightened up the legislation to keep the burden on
employers who are easier to attack than their sub-contract workers.
These additional burdens bring yet further problems to employers and
cannot improve the prospect of the small business sector helping reduce
the unemployment problem of the country.

CAPITAL GAINS TAX

There are areas in which a small change in a procedure may have a vast
change in the fiscal effect of a transaction. The law is full of booby
traps for the unwary and it is often the form rather than the substance
of an action which determines the outcome. In addition, the niceties
of interpretation which have been referred to above can mean that very
similar transactions receive different treatment either at different
times or in different tax offices.

The knowledge that these pitfalls and variations of interpretation
exist inhibit rapid decision taking which is often necessary for the
success of an undertaking. It is sometimes found that 'anti-avoidance
provisions' which are aimed at preventing one form of abuse are a
deterrent to actions which are not seeking to abuse or exploit loopholes
in the system. It is not unknown for a Tax Inspector to refuse a
clearance for a proposed action because he feels his hands are tied but
at the same time for him to be sympathetic towards the purpose behind
the proposed action. He might even propose an alternative course of
action as a way round his particular difficulty but be unaware that the
action which he sees as the easy solution will trigger difficulties in
a different part of the Inland Revenue machine.

VALUATIONS

Valuations and apportionment frequently need to be negotiated with the
Inland Revenue. In some capital gains computations a tax payer has a
choice between a valuation basis and another basis. He must make his
choice before he has an opportunity to discuss the valuation with the
Inland Revenue. Negotiations can take months or years to settle in
some cases. In smaller cases the cost of discussions and arguments
with the Departments can outweigh the amount of tax involved and the
tax payer therefore is compelled to give way to arguments and principles
with which he is not in agreement. Certain valuation departments rely
heavily on previously agreed cases as the basis for future settlements
and there is a danger than when submitting to superior force a tax
payer may not only be incurring an extra tax liability for himself but
may also be creating an undesirable precedent for himself or other tax
payers.

FUTURE REFORMS

Everybody who is closely concerned with the administration of taxation
will have views on the direction in which reform should go. Perhaps the
least contentious point that should be made is that whatever reforms
are contemplated they should be done in a way which simplifies the
system. It is acknowledged that simplification will be enormously
difficult and it is fashionable to say that simplicity and equity
normally tug in opposite directions. However over-complexity is in
itself an inequity. It is also extremely wasteful of valuable talent
and resources.

EXAMPLES

TIMING (1)

Landlord owns a building which he lets for £2,000 per annum. Very
extensive repairs become necessary. These are started in December 1981
and completed in May 1982 at which time a bill for £4,000 is received
and paid. The rent for the year to 31 March 1982 has not been paid by
the end of the year but is paid in June 1982. The rent for the year to

31 March 1983 is also received during that year.

It will be seen that during tax year 1981–82 no rent has been received but £2,000 is owing to the landlord. During the same year no expenses have been paid but at least £2,000 of the repair expenditure has accrued. During tax year 1982–83, £4,000 is received in rent and £4,000 is paid out for repairs.

The tax treatment is:

1981–82   £2,000 is assessable because the rent was due for the tax year although not received until later. No deduction is allowed for accrued expenditure on repair.

1982–83   £2,000 is assessable but against this there is an admissible deduction of £4,000, converting the income into a loss of £2,000. The loss cannot be carried back against income of earlier periods. It can be carried forward and deducted from income of later years. In the event of the expenses in later years exceeding the rents arising the benefit of loss relief will be lost.

TIMING (2)

	Company 'A'		Company 'B'	
Trading profit for year ended 31 March 1980	60,000		60,000	
Chargeable gain arising on 26 March 1980	30,000		n/a	
Tax on trading profit		27,467		24,000
Tax on chargeable gain		15,600		
Trading profit for year ended 31 March 1981	50,000		50,000	
Chargeable gain arising on 10 April 1980	n/a		30,000	
Tax on trading profit		20,000		20,000
Tax on chargeable gain				15,600
Total income and gains	140,000		140,000	
Total tax for two years		63,067		59,600

Notes:

1. In each case the gain was £52,000 but the amount chargeable was only 30/52nds of this. The chargeable gain was then taxed at the full corporation rate of 52 per cent.

2. In the year to March 1980 Company 'A' does not enjoy the full benefit of the 'small company rate' because the gain, when added to the income, takes the company above the relevant limit.

3. Company 'A' pays £3,467 more in tax than company 'B' because it was unlucky (or imprudent) enough to allow the gain to arise two weeks too early.

VOLATILITY

Two individuals have the same aggregate income over two years but do not have the same each year. They are each entitled to the same tax allowances (including mortgage interest relief).

I	Individual 'A'		Individual 'B'	
	1980–81	1981–82	1980–81	1981–82
Income	1,000	8,000	4,000	5,000
Allowances	3,000	3,200	3,000	3,200
Chargeable	nil	4,800	1,000	1,800
Tax (@ 30 per cent)	nil	1,440	300	540
Total tax for two years	£1,440		£840	

II	Individual 'C'		Individual 'D'	
	1980–81	1981–82	1980–81	1981–82
Income	5,000	22,000	12,800	14,200
Allowances	3,000	3,200	3,000	3,200
Chargeable	2,000	18,800	9,800	11,000
Tax @ 30 per cent	600	3,375*	2,940	3,300
Tax @ 40 per cent		800		
Tax @ 45 per cent		1,575		
Tax @ 50 per cent		1,025		
		6,776		
Total tax for two years	£7,375		£6,240	

* 30 per cent rate is limited to the first £11,250.

Individuals 'A' and 'C' pay more tax than 'B' and 'D' not because overall they are more prosperous but because their income arises erratically rather than consistently.

MISTRUST OF GOVERNMENT (1)

At one time there were two different rates for Value Added Tax in addition to the zero rate. This presented some businesses with the difficulty of how to record which of their sales were at which rate. The Customs and Excise Department devised special schemes for retailers. These were intended to simplify the work of keeping positive information at the point of sale. One simplified version was to look at the purchase for a period and to base the probable sales figure on the purchases with appropriate mark-ups. There was a slight danger of loss of tax to the Exchequer in adopting this rule of thumb allocation of purchases and therefore anybody who adopted it would have to pay an extra one-eighth of the tax as a safety margin.

A retailer with several shops which had a high turnover of inexperienced staff was visited by an officer of the Customs and Excise and it was explained that this system was available but that with this system there was the drawback that the extra one-eighth was added to the tax. It was said that the alternative was to keep a record of all sales at the point of sale.

Because of the cost and difficulty of instructing each sales assistant to record and classify every sale, the simplified version was accepted.

The nature of the business was such that less than 1 per cent of the turnover was zero rated and less than 1 per cent was taxable at higher rate. It was therefore possible to see that the precautionary addition of one-eighth was very excessive.

If the trader had been given the option to record all higher rate sales at the point of sale and then to assume that all other sales were at the normal rate, the department would have been fully protected against any underpayment but the burden put on the retailer would not have been anything like as arduous and costly as the burden he was told he must shoulder.

It can be shown in figures that the scheme which was adopted cost the trader over £40,000 more than the maximum liability could have been making the most unfavourable assumptions regarding the allocation of sales. This therefore was the price he had to pay as an alternative to creating very arduous and expensive extra records.

The Department did have the power to make special arrangements with traders to meet special circumstances. However, they refused to consider this power in dealing with individual traders. The only exception they made to this rule was with the NAAFI, with whom they were prepared to negotiate a separate scheme.

In saying that the retailer had the choice of recording every sale or of adopting the special scheme it is possible that the Department was wrong. If only the non-standard sales were required to be recorded, this might have met the requirements of the law. It has however, been impossible to discover the view of the Department on this matter.

The trader made a choice between the two options offered to him. It seems clear that there was a third choice that was not explained to him. It also seems clear that there was a fourth approach which the Department was empowered to make but which it refused to consider. The Department now says that the trader must accept the consequences of the choice he made.

There is no possibility of obtaining redress via the Ombudsman. The officer who explained the choices available to the trader did not act improperly. Indeed he tried his best to be helpful but his knowledge of the law was inadequate. The trader must therefore accept what is a demonstrable inequity because of a technicality in the law.

MISTRUST OF GOVERNMENT (2)

Two companies wish to make retirement provision for a director who has served for thirty years and is due for retirement.

Company A   prepares a Superannuation Fund Deed appointing a
             Trustee to receive the sum of £100,000. The Trustee
             pays £25,000 as a lump sum to the retiring director
             and hands the balance of £75,000 to Life Assurance
             Company 'X' who agree to pay the director an annuity

for life.

The Superannuation Funds Office approve the arrangement and Company 'A' is entitled to deduct the sum of £100,000 in calculating its taxable profit.

Company B   makes a payment of £25,000 to the retiring director and hands £75,000 to Life Assurance Company 'X' who agree to pay the director an annuity for life.

The arrangement is not approved because no Trustee has been appointed.   The fact that if a Trustee had been appointed he would have done exactly the same with the money as the company has done is irrelevant. It is the form, not the substance, of the arrangement which is important.

Company 'B' cannot deduct the sum of £100,000 in calculating its taxable profit.

III NEGLECTED AREAS OF SMALL BUSINESS ACTIVITY

Franchising — An Avenue for Entry into Small Business

JENSINE HOUGH

In the discussion of small business formation within the Bolton Report
(1971), franchising as a source of small business development was not
specifically examined. There has been considerable growth of franchising in Britain over the past decade, despite earlier predictions to the
contrary (Mendelsohn, 1970: 79). It provides an avenue into small
business ownership for many hardworking and determined people with
access to capital but who perhaps prefer a more 'sheltered' or ready-
made form of self-employment. By operating as a franchisee the small
businessman has the chance to own and run a business with the continuing help and backing of his franchisor.

While the roots of franchising can be traced back to late 18th century
Britain when public houses developed tied relationships with specific
breweries in return for financial assistance (Stanworth, 1977: 4), it
was in the United States that the concept was more fully developed and
exploited. The Singer Sewing Machine Company first began using franchised distributors in America soon after the Civil War. The system
then declined until the beginning of the 20th century when motor car
and soft drink syrup manufacturers began to use franchising in the distribution of their products. The system was adopted by petroleum distributors in the 1930s when they changed from wholly owned company
outlets, and they were joined by franchised drug stores, automotive
parts, food, variety goods, hardware chains and the like (Vaughn, 1979:
8, 19-21).

Franchise activities have been broadly divided into four categories
which describe the type of relationship between the parties (Vaughn,
1979: 5-9). Types 1 to 3 cover the older forms of franchising which
entail an ongoing, but generally less rigorously specified relationship
than that found in the fourth type. The first type involves a tie

between a manufacturer and his retailers commonly found in franchised car dealer networks and dealer owned petrol stations. Manufacturer-wholesaler franchises constitute the second category and are common in the soft drink industry, while the third type, wholesaler-retailer franchises, are common to the American drug store and similar chains and broadly cover many of the voluntary grocery chains found in the United Kingdom.

It is, however, the fourth type of franchising which is of prime interest as its rapid expansion in the United States over the last thirty years has been responsible for the franchise boom and much of the growth of franchising in the United Kingdom over the past ten years. This type of franchising is commonly known as business format franchising (Mendelsohn, 1979: 10) because the franchisee not only sells the franchisor's product or service (predominantly service), but does so in accordance with precisely laid down procedures. In return the franchisor provides the franchisee with assistance in carrying on his business. This includes training in the organisation and running of the business prior to opening, as well as continued advice and assistance in areas such as staff training, marketing, management assistance, research and development and the like. The franchisee usually trades under the franchisor's tradename and/or trademark and so becomes indistinguishable from a wholly owned outlet in the public's eyes. It has been suggested that in this type of franchising the franchisor is rather like a management consulting firm with a trade name to sell (Vaughn, 1979: 9), unlike the other types of franchises where the franchisor is primarily concerned with distributing his products.

In essence, then, a franchise involves a contractual relationship between the franchisor, who owns the trademark or tradename and know-how, and each of his legally independent outlets or franchisees. The franchisee, like any other small businessman, provides the capital for his business, but agrees to conduct it in accordance with the franchisor's guidelines or 'blueprint'. He usually pays both a one-off initial licence fee and some form of continuing royalty, either a percentage of turnover or a mark-up on products supplied by the franchisor. While there is no principal and agent relationship between the parties (Vaughn, 1979: 3; Mendelsohn, 1979: 27-31), the continuing financial obligation (coupled with those of standards of business conduct) and on-going

64

relationship between the parties distinguishes the franchise from many other types of business opportunity.[1]

THE SCOPE OF FRANCHISING IN THE UNITED KINGDOM

As no official statistics on franchising are collected in the United Kingdom it is difficult to ascertain the number of franchised outlets in operation or their financial contribution to the economy. However, despite franchising being a relatively little known or understood concept, many business format franchises enjoy the status of household names. These include Wimpy and Kentucky Fried Chicken (fast food), Ziebart (vehicle rustproofing), Dyno-Rod (drain cleaning), Home Tune (mobile car tuning), ServiceMaster (carpet cleaning), Prontaprint (instant printing), Pronuptia de Paris (bridal wear), Budget Rent a Car (car rentals) and Manpower (employment agency).

If one includes all the categories of business covered by statistics on franchising in the United States (Franchising in the Economy, 1981) then tied public houses, franchised car dealers, dealer-owned petrol stations and voluntary grocery chains should be added to any figures available on business format franchising when estimating its pervasiveness here. Stanworth and Curran estimated that, when these are included, the imbalance between the number of franchises in the United Kingdom and the United States is not as large as is usually assumed, especially if differences in population and market size are accounted for (Stanworth and Curran, 1978: 23, 25). The British Franchise Association, most of whose members run business format franchises, reported that by the latter part of 1981 its forty-five members had nearly 4,600 retail outlets with sales of £327.5 million (BFA, 1981).

THE SURVEY

The research on which this paper draws has been in progress since 1979, with most of the fieldwork being undertaken during 1980–81. Four established franchising companies agreed to take part, these being Home Tune, Prontaprint, Servotomic (trading as Servowarm) and Ziebart.[2]

Home Tune was established in 1968 as the country's first mobile car tuning service. It has over 100 franchisees operating more than 200

mobile units. The level of investment is modest, currently around
£5,000, as franchisees operate from their own home and their van and
equipment can be leased. Prontaprint, which operates high speed printing and instant copying shops, was established in 1971 and is expanding
rapidly. It currently has well over 100 franchisees. The typical
total investment required is around £28,000. Servotomic, however,
operates a more modestly priced franchise, with franchisees again
usually operating from their homes. Franchisees, operating under its
trade name, Servowarm, sell and install its own gas central heating
systems. Though little capital investment is required, franchisees
need approximately £6-7,000 working capital. Servotomic began franchising in 1971 in areas not economic to serve through its branch network
and has 47 franchisees. The fourth franchise, Ziebart, is a vehicle
rustproofing franchise with around 100 stations and requires an investment of £7,000 upwards, depending on whether it is added onto an existing business or not. It was established in 1970 under licence from the
United States and began franchising in 1972.

Franchisor executives and 80 franchisees (then representing a sample
of approximately one in four franchisees) from the four companies were
interviewed in depth on a variety of aspects of franchising. Taped
franchisee interviews, typically lasting around 1½ hours, were undertaken throughout Britain. Both franchisor executives and franchisees
were questioned about aspects of entry into franchising, the on-going
franchisor-franchisee relationship, contractual obligations and variations and attitudes toward committees and franchise associations. In
addition to the in-depth interview programme a mailed questionnaire
survey of around 275 franchisees who were not personally interviewed has
been undertaken. As results from this part of the research programme
are not yet available, this paper is based on the in-depth interview
survey.

Due to the wide range of aspects covered in the survey it is intended
to restrict this paper to one major aspect pertaining to franchisees
only; their socio-economic characteristics, focusing in particular on
previous work experience and educational backgrounds. These will, where
possible, be compared with other studies of small businessmen and/or
franchisees in order to ascertain how typical the respondents are as
small businessmen and what the findings add to our understanding of small

66

businessmen in the UK.

RESEARCH FINDINGS

Age and Marital Status

The entry of founder owner-managers into business ownership has been
seen as typically occuring later in life, at a time when the would-be
entrepreneur has accumulated enough capital to buy a little business
(Bechhofer and Elliott, 1978: 63). The previous franchising surveys
showed that the majority of their respondents were in their 30s or 40s
when surveyed. These studies, like the present one, bias the age of
entry upwards by reporting the age when interviewed, not when the franchise was taken. Given that the median time in business was five years
for both the present study and that by Stanworth (1977: 62), any
problems of age comparison between franchisees and small business
founders are not as acute as, for example, those in Boswell's sample of
founders (1972: 231). These had a median age of 56 when interviewed
but of 36 when they founded their firms, the median time in business
being nineteen years. Deeks' 1972 survey, like the Bolton Report's
(1971: 8) survey of chief executives, probably upwardly biased the ages
of respondents due to a non-recognition of these factors, while Bland
et al (1978) may be biased towards the younger age group by reporting
age of entry into shopkeeping, and not when starting in business as a
shopkeeper. Given these provisos there do appear to be similarities
between independent small businessmen and franchisees in the age at
which they choose to start their business venture.

There are, however, some differences exhibited between the franchises
in the present study. Ziebart respondents were most likely to be under
40 and Servowarm respondents over 40. It is difficult to generalise
about Servowarm respondents as their sample was both very small - only
ten - and selected by the franchisor. It may also be biased upward in
age by the number with prior associations with the franchisor. Ziebart
respondents were not only younger, but were also likely to exhibit
further differences to the other respondents. For example, they tended
to be better educated and were also less likely to have their spouses
involved in the business.

TABLE 1

AGE DISTRIBUTION OF SMALL BUSINESSMEN AND FRANCHISEES

	Under 30	30-39	40-49	50-59	Over 60	N=
	%	%	%	%	%	
Small Businessmen						
Bland, et al.	26	41	22	10	1	303
Boswell	32	29	32	----7----		28
Deeks	14	20	18	30	18	94
Mayer & Goldstein	18	31	28	17	5	93
Franchisees						
Ozanne & Hunt	14	26	30	21	9	933
Walker	6	25	37	24	8	288
Stanworth*	10	38	26	16	6	114
Hough – Total	4	46	25	20	5	80
– Home Tune	–	46	29	18	7	28
– Prontaprint	–	47	32	21	–	19
– Servowarm	–	20	30	40	10	10
– Ziebart	13	57	13	13	4	23

* 4% non-response

Sources: Bland, Elliott & Bechhofer (1978: 238) – Age at entry to
              shopkeeping.
           Boswell (1972: 231) – Age at founding of firm.
           Deeks (1972: 130) – Age of owner-managers when surveyed.
           Mayer & Goldstein (96: 26) – Age at founding of firm.
           Ozanne & Hunt (971: 139) – Age when surveyed.
           Walker (1971: 106) – Age when surveyed.
           Stanworth (1977: 67) – Age when surveyed.

As might be expected in a sample of this age group, ninety per cent of
franchisees in the present sample were married. This was the same proportion as in the other franchising studies, and a high proportion of
wives (over 76%) were involved in the day-to-day running of the franchise. All Home Tune and Servowarm respondents were married and, since
almost all of them conducted their businesses from home, it is not
surprising that their wives should also usually be active in the business (though their involvement varied from answering the telephone
through to undertaking the majority of administration).   These results
support Stanworth's findings, with his home based franchise, Service-
Master, having over 30 per cent more franchisees being assisted by their
spouses than in his other franchises (Stanworth, 1977: 85). Although

based outside the home, Prontaprint franchisee's wives were also very active in the business. This may have been influenced by the fact that the median period in business was only three years and that the working conditions are clean and pleasant. In contrast, conditions in Ziebart outlets tend to be very workshop like and perhaps inclined to be in more of a 'man's world'. The findings for Ziebart were similar to those reported by Stanworth (1977: 34, 36-37) for Dyno-Rod and Wimpy franchsees; both operated in separate business premises, and both having been franchising for some time. (The median time in business for Ziebart respondents was seven years.) Ziebart franchisees were less likely to be married than other respondents in the survey, and only 53 per cent involved their spouses in the running of the business, a similar proportion to those in Dyno-Rod and Wimpy.

It would appear that, at least once the franchisee's business has been established, those who operate from separate business premises and employ staff, tend to reduce the active involvement of their spouse in the every day running of the business. This is further born out by Ozanne and Hunt (1971: 144) who found that only around 56 per cent of their married fast food franchisees were assisted by their spouses. It is more difficult for a home-based franchisee's spouse to totally withdraw from active involvement with the day-to-day running of the business. At the very least she will continue to provide the first point of customer contact by taking bookings over the telephone. Withdrawal is only feasible if the business grows large enough to support a separate office or some other arrangement can be made for bookings to be taken outside the home.

Education

It is a widely held belief that small businessmen are not on the whole well educated, especially when compared with their big business counterparts (Bolton Report, 1971: 8-9; Deeks, 1972: 130-133, 136) and so may have failed in the more traditional methods of social achievement (Stanworth and Curran, 1976: 102). In their study of newly formed small firms in the United States, Mayer and Goldstein found that more than half the sample had not completed high school (1967: 25). Like the United Kingdom small businessmen reported by Deeks (1972), they were not as well educated as their big business counterparts, although better educated than the population as a whole.

Two United States studies on franchising showed franchisees to be substantially better educated than Mayer and Goldstein's small businessmen. A third of Ozanne and Hunt's (1971: 106) franchisees had graduated from college, while a half of Walker's (1971: 141) had. Ozanne and Hunt stated that their fast food franchisee sample exhibited an 'unexpectedly high level of formal education' (1971: 108) which may, however, have been partially accounted for by the better educated amongst their sample being more likely to return questionnaires. However, Walker's sample provides further evidence that American franchisees may well be better educated than their independent small business counterparts.

It is, however, difficult to compare the United States and United Kingdom educational systems directly, though it would be of interest if a similar trend in educational attainment between independent and franchised small businessmen is evident in the UK. Deeks' (1972) survey of small furniture firm owners and managers and Bland, Elliott and Bechhofer's (1978) of shopkeepers indicate a lower level of secondary school attainment amongst small businessmen than for their large firm counterparts. However, only in one of the franchises surveyed was the lack of secondary school achievement as high as was reported by Deeks. While 64 per cent of Home Tune respondents failed to gain qualifications, only 37 per cent of Prontaprint and 30 per cent of Servowarm and Ziebart respondents did so. Indeed, over a quarter (26 per cent) of Ziebart respondents had some 'A' levels.

Due to the extensive use of selection examinations at age eleven which most respondents would have been subject to, any discussion of educational attainment amongst UK small businessmen needs to consider the type of secondary school attended. Stanworth regarded his sample of franchisees as showing a high level of grammar and private school attendance, enough to make them 'certainly not typical of the population as a whole' (1977: 69). Almost half of the present sample attended grammar or private schools, a slightly higher proportion than that found by Stanworth, with a greater proportion attending grammar schools. The proportions attending grammar and private schools varied between the franchises surveyed and, in so doing, broadly reflected the proportion gaining examination passes. Over three quarters of respondents who

TABLE 2

TYPE OF SECONDARY SCHOOL ATTENDED

	Elementary/ Secondary	Grammar	Public/ Independent	Other	N=
	%	%	%	%	
Small Firms - UK					
Deeks (founders)	74	13	13	–	– **
Boswell (founders)	48	41	11	–	27
Roberts et al.	59	------41------		–	39
Franchising - UK					
Stanworth - Total	48	26	19	6*	114
– ServiceMaster	68	29	3	–	31
– Dyno-Rod	35	29	29	7*	31
– Wimpy	45	23	23	10*	52
Hough - Total	45	35	14	8	80
– Home Tune	61	32	–	7	28
– Prontaprint	26	32	37	5	19
– Servowarm	50	30	10	10	10
– Ziebart	35	44	13	8	23

* *overseas and non-response*   ** *not stated*

Sources: *Deeks, (1972: 131) founders.*
            Boswell, (1972: 230) founders.
            Roberts, et al., (1977: 113) white collar, self-employed.
            Stanworth (1977: 68)

attended grammar or private schools achieved recognised examination
passes as against only half of those who had attended either secondary
modern or comprehensive schools. Of the latter, older respondents were
less likely to have left school with recognised qualifications than
younger ones.

Amongst the present sample Ziebart respondents were the youngest, and
the most likely to have left school with qualifications. Nearly 70 per
cent did so, and those who attended secondary modern schools were far
more likely to have gained CSEs or 'O' Levels than those Home Tune or
Prontaprint respondents who had attended secondary modern schools. Comparison between respondents in different franchise systems, and between
them and other small businessmen are thus complicated by two inter-
related factors: age and changes in the educational system.

Changes in the education system, however, do not provide an adequate explanation of the whole of the variation between franchises in the present survey. Home Tune and Prontaprint respondents showed a marked divergence in success at school which cannot be accounted for by age differences. There are, however, differences in the type of school attended. Prontaprint respondents were the most likely of all respondents in the present survey to have been privately educated. While over 60 per cent of Home Tune respondents went through the lower tier of secondary education, only just over a quarter of Prontaprint respondents did so. The variation between the two samples is almost entirely accounted for by the high proportion of Prontaprint respondents who were privately educated, indicating a social as well as educational divergence.

With respect to the type of school attended and the gaining of recognised examination passes, Home Tune franchisees are closer to Stanworth's ServiceMaster franchisees than to the other respondents in the survey. These franchises are similar in that the franchisee's work has a high manual content which is unlikely to be delegated to employees, the business is usually conducted from the home and the capital requirement is modest. Similarly, Ziebart and Prontaprint respondents resemble Stanworth's Dyno-Rod and Wimpy franchisees in many ways, especially with regard to type of school attended.

The tendency to go onto further or higher education, and the type undertaken, is strongly reflected in the educational backgrounds of respondents and, as such, varies between the franchises surveyed. This variability is also reflected in the surveys of small businessmen in differing business sectors. While the use of the Bolton Committee's report for comparative purposes is restricted in that most of the respondents would have been educated prior to the second world war, it may be noted that well over half of their small business chief executives received no formal post-school qualifications at all (Bolton Report, 1971: 8-9). Somewhat to the other extreme, more than 90 per cent of Boswell's small business founders had some form of post-school further or higher educational qualifications (1972: 231). The majority of these qualifications were undertaken on a part-time basis, as was also commonly found in Deeks' furniture industry survey (Deeks, 1972: 135).

TABLE 3

POST SECONDARY SCHOOL QUALIFICATIONS

	Home Tune	Prontaprint	Servowarm	Ziebart	Total
	%	%	%	%	
Did not attempt/ not completed	29	42	60	52	44
City and Guilds	36	16	–	9	19
HNC/HND	11	11	–	13	10
Other Further*	18	21	30	13	19
Degree or above	–	5	10	13	6
Professional	4	5	–	–	3
Not known	4	–	–	–	1
	100	100	100	100	100
	N=18	N=19	N=10	N=23	N=80

* *wide variety of responses, eg: armed forces, merchant navy, teaching, etc.*

The present sample displayed quite a strong tendency to go onto further, or sometimes higher, education, and to complete their courses. This varied between the franchises surveyed, however, with Home Tune respondents, the least qualified educationally, being by far the most likely to have obtained a recognised qualification after leaving school. As has been found in other surveys of franchisees and small businessmen (see, for example, Stanworth, 1977; Deeks, 1972; Boswell, 1972), the majority of respondents obtained their qualifications part-time, either through day release or night school. It would appear that many of those who undertook post secondary qualifications did so as a consequence of the type of work they entered on leaving school.

It is notable in the present survey that all Home Tune franchisees who obtained post secondary qualifications did so on a part time basis. Further, 65 per cent of these undertook manual or technically orientated courses, and Home Tune accounted for two thirds of all respondents with City and Guilds, and nearly a third of those with HNCs or HNDs.

There seems to be a relationship between attendance at secondary modern school, failure to obtain secondary school qualifications and the subsequent obtaining of further educational qualifications within the

present sample. It may be that the lower proportion of respondents
with further educational qualifications in Stanworth's franchisee
survey is more a reflection of the type of employment entered into on
leaving school than any unwillingness to undertake it and this may also
be so for the other small business surveys.

Prior Work Experience

Studies on small businessmen in the United States have reported that
many had held lower status occupations prior to starting their businesses (Ziegler, 1979; Mayer & Goldstein, 1961: 22-23).   Over half of
Mayer and Goldstein's respondents had held only blue collar jobs prior
to starting their businesses, and a further sixteen per cent had both
blue and white collar experience. Unfortunately, the British studies
on small businessmen do not provide very clear information on prior work
experience, although it is apparent that, at least in Deeks' (1972) and
Boswell's (1972) surveys, the majority of small businessmen who go into
the manufacturing sector have a manual background.

Franchising, however, tends to be concentrated in the service industries and, as such, one might expect franchisees to have less manual
orientation than small manufacturers, except where there is a high
manual content to the work.

As might be expected, respondents' prior work experience was influe-
ced by the type of school they attended and subsequent educational
attainment. Approaching 40 per cent described their main occupation
prior to entry as manual work. With their greater likelihood of attending secondary modern school, coupled with the taking of trade qualifications, it is not surprising that Home Tune respondents were far more
likely to have had manual backgrounds than the other respondents.
Overall, however, respondents showed a tendency to move away from manual
occupations in the job they held immediately prior to taking their
franchise.

Over a third (36 per cent) of respondents' last occupations fell into
different employment categories[3] to their main occupations. The proportion of manual workers fell by a fifth, and of white collar rose 7
per cent overall. Within white collar occupations middle to upper
management groups (including semi-professionals and professionals)

TABLE 4

FRANCHISEE'S OCCUPATION IMMEDIATELY PRIOR TO ENTRY

	Manual	White Collar	Self-Employed	Misc.	N=
	%	%	%	%	
United States					
Ozanne & Hunt	13	50	26	11	916
Walker	8	76	16	–	277
United Kingdom					
Stanworth – Total	12	47	36	5	114
– ServiceMaster	19	61	16	3	31
– Dyno–Rod	10	52	36	3	31
– Wimpy	10	35	48	8	52
Hough – Total	19 (39)*	55 (48)	25 (10)	1 (3)	80
– Home Tune	36 (57)	43 (36)	21 (7)	– –	28
– Prontaprint	16 (26)	58 (69)	26 (5)	– –	19
– Servowarm	– (20)	70 (70)	30 (10)	– –	10
–Ziebart	9 (35)	70 (39)	17 (17)	4 (9)	23

* *figures in brackets refer to franchisees main occupation prior to entry.*

Sources: *Ozanne and Hunt (1971: 111, Walker (1971: 512), Stanworth (1977: 70).*

increased by more than a half and only one respondent was left in the lower white collar category. The remainder are accounted for by the greater proportion who were self-employed immediately prior to taking their franchise. To some extent, however, part of the fall within manual occupations is overstated through four Home Tune franchisees having left manual jobs to become self-employed operators for other Home Tune franchisees, work with a high manual content.

Respondents in the present survey were more likely to have been manual workers in either their last or main jobs than respondents in the other franchising studies reported in Table 4. Stanworth's ServiceMaster franchisees, who have been shown to parallel Home Tune franchisees in many other ways, were none the less far less likely to have been manual workers than Home Tune respondents. ServiceMaster did, however, have the highest proportion of respondents with manual last jobs. What is surprising amongst Home Tune respondents, however, is not the proportion who had been manual workers, but those who had not, there being a high manual content to the work they undertake as franchisees.

The main reason given by franchisees for leaving their previous employment was a desire to run their own business, mentioned by nearly a quarter. A fifth had left because they didn't like their last jobs (and presumably were, or thought they would be, unable to get suitable alternative employment). Redundancy, now a prospect facing many long term employees, was fourth on the list of reasons, with nearly an eighth of respondents falling into this group. Others left for varying reasons, for example; feeling they were being passed over or were underqualified and so unlikely to get promotion, or having a low income which was unlikely to be increased.

Table 4 indicates that a high proportion of franchisees had white collar backgrounds or prior experience in self-employment. The higher proportion of Walker's respondents with white collar backgrounds probably reflects their high educational achievement compared to other franchising respondents. As stated above, respondents in the present survey indicated a substantial shift from blue to white collar status occupations in the position held immediately prior to taking their franchise. By reporting only the last position held the other studies on franchising probably tended to underrepresent the manual backgrounds of their respondents, and thus the tendency toward upward social mobility amongst the franchisees they surveyed.[4] It has been noted elsewhere that a high proportion of small businessmen spend part of their careers in manual or lower white collar 'wage' work, and entering self-employment increases their social status. Should their business fail, however, they are most likely to return to their original employment status (Ziegler, 1979: 65; Mayer & Goldstein, 1961: 23).

Another method used to ascertain a small businessman's tendency toward upward social mobility is through examination of the type of work his father undertook. Some studies on small businessmen quote this aspect in preference to the small businessman's own prior employment history. (See, for example, Boswell, 1972; Deeks, 1972; Bechhoffer & Elliott, 1978). Stanworth (1977: 69) noted a trend toward upward social mobility between respondents and their fathers in terms of employment status, with respondents being more likely to have held white

TABLE 5
FATHERS' MAIN OCCUPATIONS

	Manual %	White Collar %	Self-Employed %	Misc. %	N=
Boswell	43	37	20	–	29
Stanworth – Total	36	26	32	7	114
– ServiceMaster	58	19	16	7	31
– Dyno–Rod	26	42	26	7	31
– Wimpy	29	20	44	8	52
Hough – Total	43	40	14	4	80
– Home Tune	54	36	4	7	28
– Prontaprint	32	48	21	–	19
– Servowarm	40	40	20	–	10
– Ziebart	39	39	17	4	23

Sources: *Boswell (1973: 230) founders' fathers*
Stanworth (1977: 68) main occupation of fathers

collar jobs. In terms of last position held, the current research
indicates similar findings. However, as respondents were asked for
their fathers' main, and not last occupation, a truer reflection may be
gained by comparing respondents' main occupational categories with
those of their fathers.

Comparison of Tables 4 and 5 show that, overall, respondents had
only a slightly lower tendency (39% to 43%) to have been manual workers
in their main occupation prior to entry into franchising than their
fathers had during their working lives. Home Tune franchisees were
slightly more likely to have been manual workers than their fathers,
while Servowarm and Prontaprint respondents' fathers were the most
likely to have been white collar workers, but not significantly so.
Examination of the white collar categories indicated that franchisees
were also less likely to have held management or professional positions
than their fathers, instead being more likely to have been salesmen. A
cross tabulation undertaken on the main categories of employment of both
respondents and their fathers revealed that less than one third fell
into the same groups. Of other respondents, 15 per cent with manual
worker fathers had held white collar main jobs and only slightly fewer
(12½%) with white collar fathers had held manual main occupations.

Comparison between Home Tune and ServiceMaster respondents' fathers again indicates similar social backgrounds between franchisees in these two low cost, manually oriented franchises. Prontaprint respondents' fathers were the least likely to have been manual workers, no doubt accounting for the fact that Prontaprint franchisees were the most likely of all respondents to have been educated at private schools, and to have had white collar main occupations prior to entry into franchising.

The fact that a franchisee has previously been involved in a business venture may not be of interest only to ascertain whether franchising has contributed to an increase in the number of small businesses in the economy. It has been found that a proportion of small businessmen, including franchisees, have a tendency to move from business to business, or to sell their business and go back into paid employment until another opportunity to go into business arises (Sklar, 1977: 44; Zeigler, 1979: 65; Mayer & Goldstein, 1961: 22-24). For instance, almost 40 per cent of Mayer and Goldstein's respondents had owned other businesses prior to their current business venture, although less than five per cent had done so exclusively.

Nearly a third (32.5%) of the present respondents had previous experience of self-employment. This ranged from working as self-employed operatives with little or no capital risk or investment to being a partner in a family owned garage chain. Those who were self-employed immediately prior to taking their franchise fell into three almost equal groups - those who had been mainly self-employed during their working lives, those who had held manual jobs and those with white collar jobs. Like the small businessmen reported in the American studies, respondents showed a tendency to move from one business to another, or even to go back into paid employment after having run a business. A quarter of respondents were self-employed immediately prior to taking their franchise. However, the transitory nature of their ventures into business is evident by the length of time they had their businesses. For instance, over a half had been self-employed for only one or two years, and a further fifth for only three to five years. Only 30 per cent (8) of those with self-employment experience stated their main occupation to have involved self-employment, and most of these were no longer involved with their previous businesses. Additionally, over a quarter

of those who had been self-employed had gone back into paid employment
before taking on their franchises.   Only one respondent had any prior
experience of franchising, however, and then not of business format
franchising.

Reasons for ceasing to operate previous businesses or for leaving
self-employment varied. The inability to make a profit was the largest
single factor, with a desire to become a fully fledged franchisee
instead of a self-employed operative or salesman within their present
franchise system the next in importance. Overall levels of previous
experience in self-employment are fairly similar throughout the various
franchising surveys reported. For the present study, however, Table 4
underestimates the prior self-employment history of respondents by
nearly 8 per cent, the proportion who had transitory experience of self-
employment and had then gone back into paid employment before taking
their franchise. Given this tendency, it is possible that the other
franchising studies (eg. Ozanne & Hunt, 1971; Walker, 1971; Stanworth,
1977) underestimate the proportion of respondents with some prior experience of self-employment. They also probably overestimate its
importance in their career histories, however, given the short time most
respondents in the present survey had been self-employed immediately
prior to taking their franchise.

Stanworth (1977: 71-73) speculated as to the likelihood of a franchisee having been both previously self-employed and having a self-
employed father. However, only around an eighth of his respondents fell
into this category. He did find that over half (55%) had been previously
exposed to self-employment before taking their franchise either through
their own self-employment and/or that of their father. Nearly 45 per
cent of respondents in the present survey stated that their father had,
at some time, been self-employed. However, only 14 per cent said that
their fathers had been mainly self-employed during their working careers.
In all approximately 18 per cent of respondents had been both previously
self-employed at some time and had fathers who had also. This is a not
insignificant proportion of respondents, and falls within roughly the
same band, albeit somewhat higher, that Stanworth found. While there
was inter-franchise variability on this aspect, ranging from only 7 per
cent of Home Tune franchisees to 30 per cent of Servowarm's, the proportion of respondents with first hand experience of self-employment

through their own experience, or that of their father, was almost constant over the four franchises surveyed, at around 57 per cent, and similar to that found overall by Stanworth.

The respondents, like Stanworth's, had mainly engaged in very small scale business ventures, although at least one had sold a larger business in favour of becoming a 'one man band' because he had grown weary of poor quality staff. It has already been noted that five respondents had worked on a self-employed basis for other franchisees or their franchisor immediately prior to taking their franchise. A further ten respondents also came from within their own franchise systems, nine having been employed by their franchisor and one having taken over the business of the franchisee who had employed him. Thus, in all fifteen respondents (19%) had direct prior experience of their franchise before becoming a franchisee.

SUMMARY AND CONCLUSIONS

Consideration of the socio-economic characteristics of small business franchisees suggests a relationship between social background and type of small business franchise entered into. There is, for instance, evidence of a relationship between type of secondary school attended, level of academic achievement and the amount of capital expended on entry into franchising. Respondents in the lower cost franchises were the most likely to have had manual worker fathers and to have been mainly employed as manual workers themselves before taking up their franchise. They usually went through the lower tier of secondary education but seemed to make up for a lack of secondary school qualifications by going onto further education. Conversely, respondents in the highest cost franchise were the most likely to have had white collar fathers, to have been previously employed in white collar jobs themselves and have had a private education.

A tendency toward upward social mobility prior to entry into franchising has been indicated by comparisons between respondent's main and last jobs. Those whose last job was not their main job had typically taken higher status jobs or become self-employed. However, there was little evidence of upward social mobility between respondents and their fathers, at least when main rather than last jobs held were compared.

Comparison between respondents' last jobs and their fathers' main job
does not necessarily provide an accurate indication of upward social
mobility between the generations. There was some evidence during interviews that fathers, like respondents, could have held different and
upwardly mobile last occupations compared with their main occupations.

Upward social mobility amongst small businessmen may, in the long run,
be more apparent than real, depending on the length of time they continue in business and whether they go back to their original employment
status should they cease to trade. The tendency of many small business
men to make several ventures into self-employment has been noted in
the United States (Sklar, 1977; Mayer & Goldstein, 1961; Zeigler,
1979) and has been evident amongst a proportion of respondents in this
survey. The majority of those who had previously been self-employed
had, however, done so for quite short periods, as had many of those
fathers with histories of self-employment. Well over half the respondents had experience of self-employment either on their own account and/
or via their fathers. Given the somewhat transitory nature of the
self-employment the majority had been exposed to, however, a franchise
may have appeared an attractive risk reducing mode of entry (or re-
entry) into business.

In the last section of their Report the Bolton Committee concluded
that '... the small firm sector is in a state of long term decline,
both in size and in its share of economic activity' (1971: 342). It
would appear that franchising has been operating against this decline.
While it is apparent that a proportion of franchisees would have gone
into business for themselves without the backing or business opportunity provided by the franchisor, there were undoubtedly many who lacked
the skills or confidence to do so. By providing the opportunity for
entry into small business for those people, franchising has contributed
to the growth of the small business sector. That one respondent felt
that 'franchising is a good way to start in business, but I'm not sure
it's a good way to finish' should not be taken as a negative aspect of
franchising. Some franchisees will be content to say in their franchise for as long as their businesses remain profitable. Others will use
it as a first step toward independent business ownership, perhaps sell-
ing their franchise and investing in another business of their own
initiation or, as some have already done, using their profits and/or

credit worthiness to diversify into complementary types of business.

In conclusion, it should be noted that the findings presented in this paper represent only one aspect of the research undertaken. Further analysis of the in-depth interview programme and results from the mailed survey sent to the remainder of franchisees in the participating franchises should further clarify the trends indicated.

ACKNOWLEDGEMENT

The author would like to acknowledge the support given by the SSRC (Project Number HR 7310/1) in funding the fieldwork on which this paper is based, and to thank Professor John Stanworth, project director, and Dr James Curran, Reader in Sociology, Kingston Polytechnic, for their help and support with the research on which this paper is based, and particularly for their comments on the drafts of this paper.

NOTES

[1.] Various types of 'business opportunity' exist where an individual may invest his own funds in order to become, for example, an agent, distributor or licensee. Many coin operated laundrettes, for example, fall into this category (Ozanne and Hunt, 1971).

[2.] At the time of the in-depth survey, Home Tune had 116 franchisees, Prontaprint 65, Servotomic 48 and Ziebart 98. A total of 88 franchisees were approached, of which 80 accepted, a 91% acceptance rate, and approximated a one in four sample.

[3.] Employment categories used were: unskilled, semi-skilled, skilled manual, lower white collar, armed forces, salesman, self-employed, middle management/semi professional, upper management/professional.

[4.] Stanworth's Table 24 here is headed 'Main Occupations of Franchisees Prior to Entry into Franchising'. It should read 'Franchisee's Last Full Time Occupation Prior to Entry Into Franchising'.

REFERENCES

Bechhofer, F., and Elliott, B., 'The Voice of Small Business and the Politics of Survival', *The Sociological Review*, Vol.26, No.1, February 1978.

Bland, R., Elliott, B., and Bechhofer, F., 'Social Mobility in the Petite Bourgeoisie', *Acta Sociologica*, Vol.21, No.3, 1978.

Boswell, J., *The Rise and Decline of Small Firms*, Allen and Unwin, 1972.

British Franchise Association, Press Release, December 1981.

Deeks, J., 'Education and Occupational Histories of Owner-Managers and Managers', *The Journal of Management Studies,* May 1972.

Franchising in the Economy, 1978-1981, U.S. Department of Commerce/ Bureau of Industrial Economics, January 1981.

Mayer, K.B. and Goldstein, S., *The First Two Years: Problems of Small Firms Growth and Survival,* Small Business Administration, Washington D.C., 1961.

Mendelsohn, M., *The Guide to Franchising,* Pergamon Press, First Edition, 1970, Second Edition, 1979.

Ozanne, U.B. and Hunt, S.D., *The Economic Effects of Franchising,* Select Committee on Small Business, United States Senate, 1971.

Roberts, K., Cook, F.G., Clark, S.C. and Semeonoff, E., *The Fragmentary Class Structure,* Heinemann, 1977.

Sklar, F., 'Franchisees and Independence', *Urban Life,* Vol.6, No.1, April 1977.

Small Firms - Report of the Committee of Inquiry on Small Firms, London, Cmnd. 4811, HMSO, 1971 (The Bolton Report).

Stanworth, J. and Curran, J., 'Franchising at a Major Crossroads', *Marketing Magazine,* April 1978.

Stanworth, M.J.K., *A Study of Franchising in Britain - A Research Report,* Polytechnic of Central London, School of Management Studies, July 1977.

Stanworth, M.J.K. and Curran, J., 'Growth and the Small Firm - an alternative view', *Journal of Management Studies,* Vol.13, No.2, May 1976.

Vaughn, C.L., *Franchising: its nature, scope, advantages and developments,* Second Edition, Lexington Books, D.C. Heath, 1979.

Walker, B.J., *An Investigation of Relative Overall Position and Need Gratification Among Franchised Businessmen,* PhD Thesis, Faculty of the Graduate School of Business Administration, University of Colorado, 1971.

Zeigler, H., *The Politics of Small Business,* Arno Press, New York, 1979.

Co-operatives in Contemporary Britain
PAUL CHAPLIN

Worker co-operatives did not rate a mention in the Bolton Report, 1971.
Ten years later it is difficult not to notice their presence. As well
as the many new ones which have become established there is a fast
growing number of training programmes, national and local development
agencies and research projects, all designed specifically with workers
co-operatives in mind.

It is a surprise, then, to realise that the number of people employed
in co-operatives is only 3–4,000 more than in 1971 and only 1–2,000
more than in 1975–6.   The explanation lies in the changing composition
of the sector. There are now ten to fifteen times as many co-operatives
as ten years ago but some of those which have disappeared were large
employers whereas most of the new ones are too young to have grown much.
In another ten years time the total employment may be considerably
greater.

DEFINITIONS

Defining a workers co-operative is not easy because neither in the
United Kingdom nor elsewhere in the world is there a legal definition.
In principle a workers co-operative is a business owned and controlled
by those who work in it. Officially only those businesses which are
registered as co-operatives with the Registrar of Friendly Societies
under the 1965 Industrial and Provident Societies Acts can call themselves co-operatives and claim the tax benefits available (all profits
taxed at the lower rate of corporation tax irrespective of their size).
In practice any business can run itself co-operatively, enshrining
democratic rules if it wishes in its Secondary Rules, Articles of Association or other internal agreement among the workers and/or others
involved.   A good number of the smaller co-operatives are unincorpor-

ated and legally would be treated as partnerships.

The main purpose of registering as a co-operative is to guarantee that it stays such. Other arrangements are easier to convert back to conventional structures should members change their minds or be replaced by others with different ideas.

In identifying co-operative businesses it is usual to rely on the fundamental principles promoted for decades by the International Co-operative Alliance. These are employed by the Registrar when considering the registration of any new business. Certain of these, such as provision for education of the workers, and co-operation between co-operatives, whilst accepted as desirable would no longer be considered central by most observers today. The rest are fundamental:

a) One person, one vote: co-operatives are democratically controlled. A member's say must be related to his participation in the business, not to his financial investment in it.

b) Open membership: anyone satisfying the co-operative's own membership qualifications must be able to join. Each co-operative can choose its own criteria, often including a probationary period as employee and/or a vote of acceptance from existing members, but these criteria must not be so prohibitive that most new people cannot join.

c) Limited return on capital: where members have shares or make loans the return on them is restricted. The rate is usually pegged to that operating in the general financial market at any time, and in some cases may be no more than 3 per cent above that rate.

d) Rewards according to participation: with the exception of those co-operatives which allow differential share-holdings (in such cases there is a maximum number of shares any member can hold, and the dividend payments are rigidly delimited) all payments from the annual surplus (i.e. profits) to members must be according to their involvement in the business (e.g. hours worked and/or pay) - how this is calculated is largely discretionary.

Everything else is open to choice. Consequently there is a great variety of particular rules. Some confusion results when certain businesses are on the border. For example some allow outside share-holders (often ex-workers). Others give additional bonuses and voting shares for each year worked in them, allowing greater influence to the longest serving members. Others build in security of position to individual managers or weight decision-making power in favour of managers generally.

The vast majority of co-operative employees, however, belong to businesses with one of two types of constitution. By far the most popular nowadays are Common Ownerships. These restrict membership to workers in the enterprise only, restrict shareholding to £1.00 per member and, as the name suggests, hold all business assets in common. In the event of dissolution any assets remaining after all liabilities have been met must be given to charity or another Common Ownership.

The majority of co-operatives in 1971 were Producer Co-operatives. These reflect the constitution developed in the last century during the original growth of worker co-operatives. They allow each member to hold up to 5,000 shares of £10 each. They allow non-workers (usually ex-employees, trade unions or similar) to hold shares. These do represent a claim on a proportion of the company's net worth.

MAIN EVENTS, CHANGES AND TRENDS

When the Bolton Committee reported there were perhaps thirty-five co-operatives employing 3,500 people. Three-quarters were Producer Co-operatives, the median age of which was sixty-one years. None were younger than twenty years. Together they employed 70 per cent of all co-operative workers. By far the biggest Common Ownership was Scott Bader, the first such and the inspiration for the whole Common Ownership movement.

Scott Bader was a privately owned resin manufacturing company employ-ing over a hundred people when in 1951 Ernest Scott Bader began its conversion to the new structure of his own creation. To promote and assist others to do the same he founded the Society for Democratic Control of Industry. In 1971 this was re-named the Industrial Ownership Movement (ICOM).

The same year witnessed the first of over a hundred factory sit-ins and work-ins that occurred in the period 1971-4 following the

inspirational example of Upper Clyde Shipbuilders. The first of these
to lead to the formation of a co-operative was Fakenham Enterprises in
Norfolk in 1972. Some of the women made redundant from the closure of
a large shoe factory set up on their own with considerable financial
help and advice from Scott Bader among others, to make parts of shoes
and other leather goods.

Then in 1974 began Tony Benn's period in the Department of Employment.
Against the resistance of his own civil servants he provided Government
start-up finance for three of the major sit-ins - Scottish Daily News
which folded after six months, Kirkby Manufacturing and Engineering Ltd.
which finally closed in May 1979, and Meriden Motorcycles which is still
employing some four hundred people. The demise of the first two with
the attendant loss of some 1,100 jobs is a major reason why the net gain
in co-operative employment over the last five years seems so low.

Many people still identify the co-operative sector with these three
businesses, usually uncharitably. Some berate them for not being
genuine co-operatives, others for wasting Government money with un-
commercial approaches. It is worth remembering that all were created
primarily to save jobs; all inherited unprofitable factories and/or
unsuccessful products which for years conventional management had failed
to convert into viable ones. Furthermore, by most independent judge-
ments all were considerably under-financed from the outset and the net
effect of the publicity they received was, contrary to popular belief,
harmful to their business. Obviously there have been faults in their
organisation as well but in the circumstances it was no mean feat for
e.g. KME to maintain eight hundred people in employment while in the
same town and during the same four year period twenty factories of
similar or larger size closed with loss of all jobs. Nor is it an in-
considerable achievement for Meriden to soldier on as the country's only
motorcycle manufacturer when five years ago the industry had been given
up for dead.

The sit-ins and work-ins were a symptom of growing unemployment which
even then was becoming a major issue. One of Government's responses
was the Manpower Services Commission's Job Creation Programme (JCP).
In the mid 1970s nearly thirty training workshops received two years
funding under the Special Temporary Employment Project (STEP) with the
opportunity to continue as independent co-operatives thereafter. In

fact only a quarter of the workshops continued when funding ceased.
Some of these have subsequently disappeared. Again there are various
causes. Rosemary Rhoades (1980) offers in her critique of the Milkwood
Co-operative two of the most prominently and frequently mentioned:

a) the limitations imposed on JCP funding militated against
   the achievement of objectives other than the employment
   of the unemployed; certainly they were not encouraging
   for new business formation.

b) the requirement for (respectable) sponsors usually meant
   that the founders were not workers in the co-operatives
   but outsiders wanting other people to carry out their own
   dreams.

Political pressure from ICOM bore fruit in 1976 with the passing, as
a Private Member's Bill with all-Party support, of the Industrial
Common Ownership (ICO) Act. This released £250,000 of Government money
over a period of five years to Industrial Common Ownership Finance Ltd.
(ICOF) for loans to manufacturing enterprises satisfying the conditions
of Common Ownership as laid down in the Act. ICOF had been established
by ICOM in 1973 specifically to operate a revolving loan fund for co-
operatives. By 1980 some £350,000 was on loan to 45 co-operatives.

The ICO Act also released for a similar period a total grant of
£30,000 per annum to help organisations set up to advise Common Ownerships. This was divided between the Scottish Co-operatives Development
Committee and ICOM. In the following year ICOM published its Model
Rules. Condensed into four pages this very simple document suddenly
made registration a much easier, quicker and cheaper procedure than
before. Now 80-90 per cent of all ICOM's trading members use ICOM Model
Rules, and up to 95 per cent of new co-operatives register with them.

In the background were developing a number of parallel but not con-
vergent strands of thought, all having some bearing on the subsequent
growth of interest in co-operatives. A groundswell of people interested
in 'alternative' life styles and non-conventional organisations were
beginning to translate their ideas into practice, bolstered by the
pervasive influence of the ideas included in 'Small is Beautiful' the
seminal work published in 1973 by E.F. Schumacher who also happened to
be on the Board of Trustees at Scott Bader.

The Institute of Workers Control (IWC), founded in 1968 and counting among its leading supporters none other than Tony Benn, was producing a constant stream of books and articles about workers control.   Philosophically rooted in the class politics of the labour movement the IWC was arguing for a labour-managed economy, not necessarily the same thing as an economy containing a third sector of co-operatives which are middle-class led and have little or no unionisation and would feel bruised by the experience of the three Benn co-operatives.   It would be much more in agreement with such initiatives as that of the Lucas Aerospace Combine Shop Stewards Committee which for years has attempted to pressurise the company to save jobs and at the same time produce socially useful products.

This trend, allied with changes in the pattern of collective bargaining (major decisions moving in companies away from individual plants to head offices), produced pressure in the trade union movement for union representation at Board level since this was where decisions to close factories were being taken.   A resolution to this effect passed at the Trades Union Congress Conference in 1974 led to the establishment of the Bullock Committee which reported in 1977.   Its central recommendation was that all sizeable companies should have single tier Boards sitting on which would be a minority of elected worker directors.   Although sometimes mistaken for worker co-operatives such companies would have been quite different.   In fact the report had little or no effect on company structure.   (In practice the experience of larger co-operative businesses suggests that a two tier Board structure might work better).

At about the same time information was beginning to pour into the country about the Mondragon co-operatives in Basque Spain.   A report published by the Anglo-German Foundation (1977) produced a glittering success story of growth from nothing to seventy co-operatives employing 15,000 people, all part of a wider co-operative system incorporating schools, colleges, farming, welfare and a central bank, and all in little more than twenty years.   This touched off a lively argument about the reasons for this success, and whether or not the values and structures could be imported from Mondragon to the United Kingdom with the same effect.   The main component of the Mondragon constitution that was seized upon is the requirement of all new co-operative members to contribute substantially (up to £2,000), which contribution would be

adjusted in relation to the profit or loss of the business each year,
the accumulated sum being withdrawable only if the worker leaves. This
is very different from the ideas both of the labour movement and ICOM.
Accordingly its proponents established their own promotional organisation, Job Ownership Limited (JOL) in 1978.   To date one co-operative
has been started (in 1981) in this country which employs the ideas
supported by JOL.

In 1978 the Inner Urban Areas Act empowered local authorities to make
grants of £1,000 for start-up expenses for new co-operatives, and the
national Co-operative Development Agency (CDA) was established with
Department of Industry funding at the rate of £300,000 per annum.   This
has been extended for a further two years from 1981 following a total
change of the members of the board and a significant reorganisation
internally.   While the CDA is better known, the autonomous local CDA's,
usually set up by local co-operatives and/or at the initiative of Local
Councils, have been of more profound importance in encouraging new co-
operatives.   ICOM's central staff have observed that new registrations
are located in disproportionate concentrations in areas known to enjoy
the services of an effective local organisation.   The same conclusion
is offered by statistics from the Directory of Co-operative Firms in
London (London ICOM, 1981).   Whereas those boroughs with full time CDA
workers have witnessed more than 100 per cent growth in trading co-operatives over the last 12-18 months, during the same period co-operatives
in other boroughs have increased by less than 50 per cent.

THE CO-OPERATIVE SCENE: A BRIEF SURVEY

The ICOM 'Directory of Common Ownership Enterprises' (1980) listed 206
fully paid up trading members of ICOM.   Most but not quite all are
bona fide Common Ownerships.   Another 50-60 had registered as members
before but had not kept up to date with subscriptions.   It is quite
likely that a proportion of these were nevertheless still trading at
the time.   Subsequently new registrations have been received at the rate
of 2-3 a week.   The trading members of ICOM therefore number in the
region of 300-350 in late 1981.

A short while after ICOM published its directory the Co-operative
Development Agency published its own (CDA, Autumn 1980).   This lists

330 co-operative enterprises, of whatever constitution, known to be operating at the time. A further 67 were legally alive but in practice untraceable. A third source is 'In the Making' an annual directory concentrating on informal and/or unincorporated enterprises. Combining the information from all three the total number of co-operatives operating in mid-1980 is estimated between 350 and 400. Given the number of known formations since, that number would now be 500-550.

The pattern of registration over time is vividly illustrated in Table 1. Particularly clear is the sudden growth starting in the middle of the decade. Table 2 reveals the geographical location although obviously the boundaries drawn are fairly arbitrary. Almost all those in London and the Home Counties are actually within the boundary of Greater London. London ICOM's membership alone has increased by 76 per cent in the last fifteen months or so. It is quite likely therefore that the number of co-operatives in this region is now 140-150.

Eighty six per cent of all co-operatives in 1980 had fewer than nineteen workers; of these 72 per cent were ICOM members. Eleven per cent of all co-operatives had between 20 and 99 workers; 40 per cent of these were ICOM members, 65 per cent had been started since the Bolton Committee reported. Three per cent of all co-operatives had a hundred or more workers; only two of these were ICOM members. Of the ten largest co-operatives seven were Producer Co-operatives, all at least fifty years old. One (Meriden) was a 'defensive' co-operative constructed out of a factory closure during the middle years of the decade. The other two, both the ICOM members, were converted from conventional ownership and control by the managing directors at the time, one as long ago as 1951, the other in the late 1970s.

Looking at the scene as a whole perhaps 5 per cent of all co-operatives derive from plant closures; together they provide about 10 per cent of total employment. Conversions like Scott Bader account for a similar proportion of co-operatives but perhaps 20 per cent of total employment. The Producer Co-operatives, now only about fifteen in number, still employ 25 per cent of those working in co-operatives. This means that new self-start co-operatives account for more than 85 per cent of all co-operatives but so far provide only 45 per cent of total employment. (All figures must perforce be approximations.)

TABLE 1

YEAR OF REGISTRATION - CO-OPERATIVES TRADING IN 1980

Year(s) of Registration	Number of Co-operatives still Trading	
1981	(Estimate)	150
1980	(Estimate)	85 (49 in first seven months)
1979		51
1978		72
1977		31
1976		28
1975		2
1970–74		17
1960s		4
1950s		3
1940s		2
1920–39		3
1900–19		5
1800s		9

Note: *Totals between Tables 1 and 2 do not exactly tally because of ambiguous or incomplete entries, and/or the same or federated co-operatives trading under different names.*

Source: *'Co-ops: A Directory of Industrial and Service Co-operatives' - CDA, Autumn 1980.*

TABLE 2

GEOGRAPHICAL LOCATION OF CO-OPERATIVES IN 1980

Area	Number of Co-operatives Trading
London & Home Counties	89
South East	7
South and South West	17
Midlands and Wales	85
North West and Northern Ireland	40
North (incl. Yorkshire) & North East	47
Scotland	26

Source: *'Co-ops: A Directory of Industrial and Service Co-operatives' - CDA, Autumn 1980*

The picture then is of rapid recent growth in new co-operative registrations, most of them adopting ICOM constitutions, most of them remaining small. None of the co-operatives which started totally anew in the last decade have yet grown to employ as many as one hundred. This is hardly surprising and quite consistent with the growth problems of businesses created e.g. through New Enterprise Programmes. What is significant is that over half of those employing 20-99 (some already employing 80 or 90 each) are less than ten years old and in the next decade some of these can be expected to continue to grow.

CO-OPERATIVES' SURVIVAL RATE

Of key interest, of course, is the relative success or survival rate of co-operatives. Derek Jones concluded that Producer Co-operatives (at least in the leather and footwear industry he studied) have a better survival rate than similar conventional businesses (Coates, 1976). The very recent London ICOM Directory records eight known collapses in the last eighteen months out of sixty-seven that were operating in 1980 (i.e. 8 per cent per annum) (London, ICOM, 1981).

More comprehensive figures are available thanks to the excellent work of Beverley Aston (1980). Linking her findings with the statistics available in the CDA Directory and those from the recent London ICOM Directory, the figures suggest that in the order of 30 per cent of all new start co-operatives for one reason or another cease trading within their first four years. The nearest comparable statistics for con- ventional businesses show that of those firms which failed in 1978, 53.2 per cent were under five years old (Scott, 1980). In general terms, then, co-operatives do appear to survive at least as well, probably better, than conventional companies.

This is achieved at some cost, however. The great majority of new co-operatives are 'alternatives' in one way or another and tend to pay their members low wages to avoid commercial failure. Beverley Aston analysed the submitted Annual Returns of a large number of alternative co-operatives. The figures are seriously depressed because she has aggregated all returns for the years 1976-80 since so many co-operatives had submitted returns erratically. Clearly this will take no account of inflation which during that period was running at an all time high.

Furthermore some returns are deceptive. Until recently all co-operatives were obliged to have a minumum of seven members although in fact only one or two of these may have been full time employed. The income per actual worker in such co-operatives therefore is likely to be much higher than the apparent income per member.

Her figures show an average salary per member among these co-operatives of £785. Taking the above points into account one estimate is that this would translate into a salary equivalent of £2,000 or so at today's values. Only one quarter of all wholefood shops were paying average wages of over £1,000 per annum and only one eighth of bookshops. Among the printing co-operatives (most of which are fully unionised) the average pay was £1,500 per annum, and among language schools £3,500 per annum.

Out of a sample of eighty-eight alternative co-operatives fifty-four were recording a profit. Most looked financially weak with an Acid Test ratio ranging from an average of 0.42 (bookshops) to 0.995 (printers), largely because of their relatively high dependence on loan finance in the form of unsecured interest free loans, usually from the members themselves, often in the form of deferred wage payments. In some sectors the average co-operative depended on such loans to the value of up to four times the average annual wage.

Many of these statistics are crude, and the standard deviations are very large. There are some financially strong, profitable alternative co-operatives paying good wages to its workers. There are others offering the opposite in every respect. Some co-operators do not want high wages anyway. Their disenchantment with the world of conventional business includes the dismissal of high incomes. Nevertheless the survival rate of alternative co-operatives clearly owes something to the willingness of their members for whatever reason to accept lower than average wages.

This undoubtedly has a lot to do with the ambivalence shown towards worker co-operatives by many unions and unionists. It also contributes to the perception of Jenny Thornley that:

'There can be no doubt about the fact that the co-operatives sector is tiny, weak, unbusinesslike and middle class, and is characterised by sweatshops' (Thornley, 1981: 173).

Most of these arguments revolve around the 'alternative' end of the co-operative spectrum. Most people involved at this end are relatively young, well educated and disillusioned with conventional party politics. At the other end the story is much more hopeful in terms of business growth and solidity. The remaining seventeen Producer Co-operatives have a combined turnover of £11½ million and almost all make solid profits. All are in old established industries. Usually they are working class, highly unionised, but ominously on a gradual decline. The other particularly stable group are the six companies which have converted to Common Ownership. These employ well over 1,000 workers between them and have a combined turnover of over £20 million per annum. One is in catering, another in jewellery retailing, a third is in the building trade, the others are in process industry or batch manufacturing. Philosophically they are quite different from the Producer Co-operatives, almost invariably inspired by Christian Socialist ideals of their founders who see co-operatives as a third way in the mixed economy, not as part of the labour movement's struggle against the prevailing economic order.

It is arguable that in time the larger more successful co-operatives, engaged in conventionalised activities and usually paying above average wages, will have the greater significance in influencing general attitudes. There are some very impressive success stories. Scott Bader remains market leader in its field despite thin times recently. Northampton Industrial Commonwealth has grown to eighty workers in five of the worst years ever in the building industry. Kennington Office Cleaners Co-operative has grown to twenty members in three years. Most of them are mothers, a good number are black, and all are receiving better pay than they were, or their colleagues still are, in conventionally owned firms in what has always been an exploitative trade. At the alternative end of the spectrum one cannot fail to be impressed by the growth of the Federation of Northern Wholefood Co-operatives which appears to have captured a dominant share of its market. It arose from the foundation of Suma, the wholefood wholesalers in Leeds, in 1975. Now Suma has a workforce of 16-20 and a turnover of £1½-2 million created from its distribution to over fifty wholefood shops. These co-operate on prices and other issues with Suma to the mutual benefit of all.

The greatest expansion is in the service sector; 70.6 per cent of all co-operatives registered in 1980 were in this sector. Service enterprises are the easiest to organise democratically - the jobs required are less distinct and less separated by skill or location. Service businesses also require less capital and most co-operatives have a particularly weak capital base.

Many co-operatives are started by people who could not or would not start a conventional business. However, unless co-operatives receive some positive discrimination in at least some of the major industries or activities they run the danger of being permanently confined within the low wage, labour intensive, marginal sectors of the economy. If anything the recent interest of larger corporations in co-operatives (and other small businesses) reinforces the trend, which implicitly reserves the large capital accumulations and investments for themselves while stimulating small scale employment and business activity at local levels as a necessary prop for their own continued trading success.

COMPARISONS WITH OTHER PLACES AND OTHER TIMES

The resurgence of interest in co-operatives is occurring everywhere in Europe, but the British movement is weaker than almost anywhere else in the continent. France has twice the number of co-operatives (many located in Brittany), six times the number of workers and much stronger central organisation and co-operative bank. In Italy where co-operatives are very firmly rooted within the labour movement there are thousands of co-operatives belonging to three federations, each with their own training, research and contracts departments. The federations put together consortia of co-operatives jointly to tender for large contracts. They also play a major part themselves in starting rather than merely registering new co-operatives which sometimes number as many as a hundred per month.

Western Europe includes 19 per cent of the known workers co-operatives in the world, 37 per cent of co-operative membership and 95 per cent total turnover. Seventy-five per cent of all members are in the Eastern Block where the Communist governments offer strong support, particularly for co-operatives with social objectives (e.g. employment of disabled people, of women, and in rural areas). In Yugoslavia self-management

97

became a cornerstone of the constitution drawn up by Tito in 1948. Subsequently self-managed business enterprises played a major part in the rapid economic development of that country. Within the last decade some cracks have been appearing: the national rate of economic growth has slowed down; unemployment has been increasing but self-managed enterprises prove reluctant to take on more workers, preferring higher wages for themselves instead. There has been an increase of strikes (most of them short lived) and the influence of managers within enterprises has been steadily growing to such an extent that the Party has attempted to intervene more itself to promote democracy.

Nevertheless, a major survey of research into Yugoslav self-management (Garson, 1974) was able to conclude that the Yugoslav system's pay structure remains more egalitarian than almost any other developed or undeveloped country. Garson judges that the self-management organs do constitute a useful check on managerial prerogatives in conflict situations although the lack of provision for independent experts to help workers councils could be a recipe for generating class divisions (and class conflict of interests) between managers and workers.

Wherever one looks a few key factors appear essential for the success of a co-operative sector. One, which is quite uncontrollable, is the pre-existence of a national or local mood of independence from, or defiance towards, central Government or some other source of potential control. This exists among the Spanish Basques and among their near cousins in Brittany. Yugoslavia enjoys or suffers both a nationalistic rejection of Soviet domination and internally cross-cutting conflicts between different nationalities. Such feelings within the United Kingdom are only likely to occur in Scotland, perhaps the North East and possibly North Wales, but if so in a relatively weak form.

Other important factors are the availability of specialist banking facilities for co-operatives and Government support in the form of tax concessions, enabling legislation and the direct offer of work. In Italy and France particularly co-operatives are favoured for certain Government building contracts. No such relationship exists here, nor does the much larger retail co-operative sector recognise workers co-operatives as sufficiently important to warrant the effort to establish strong commercial links. Perhaps worker co-operatives are themselves much to blame for this. If they were to produce the sort of goods needed in quantity by the other co-operative sectors (including agricultural and housing) the establishment of such links might follow quite quickly.

Some interesting issues are raised by a different set of comparisons. The essentially middle class character of most contemporary co-operatives has already been identified, as has the growth in numbers of new co-operatives since the introduction of ICOM Model Rules. It is tempting to find the parallels between this phase of growth and that which led to the establishment of the original Producer Co-operative sector. Up to 1982, although a strong and organised movement was emerging, the number of Producer Co-operatives created remained quite small. The formation of the Co-operative Productive Federation in 1882 presaged a decade of much more vigorous expansion when the number of co-operatives increased sixfold. Thereafter growth in terms of new co-operatives gradually slowed down while the established ones grew larger. One wonders whether the introduction of ICOM Model Rules has not introduced a similar and temporary spurt of growth although clearly there are many other different factors involved too.

The inference from the second set of comparisons is just as tenuous, and just as intriguing. In reviewing the history of the British co-operative movement G.D.H. Cole (1945) concluded that the early co-operatives were dominated by, and provided most benefit to, the lower middle classes. Only when general economic conditions improved did members of the working class join the co-operative movement in force. Quite the opposite from what would be expected, then, co-operatives were not the agent of improvement of the standard of living of the poorest people but themselves benefitted when other factors independently improved the lot of these people. There is a somewhat bizarre but very pervasive parallel in most Third World countries today where co-operatives, where they have been successful, have tended to increase rather than decrease the differences in power both between men and women and between the poorest in the community and those with at least a little property and income. Co-operatives have improved the position of the middle classes relative to that of the wealthiest but done little for the poorest. Both historical examples provide a warning about how much social change workers co-operatives can achieve and the direction of possible future trends. It is noticeable too that in Britain today it

is the mainly middle class Social Democratic Party/Liberal Party
Alliance which is by far the most comfortable in supporting co-operatives. Nevertheless this trend is far from inevitable as the movements
in France and Italy demonstrate.

PARTICULAR ISSUES FACING CO-OPERATIVES

Finance

The weak financial base of many co-operatives has already been touched
on.   Very few co-operatives start up with much initial cash investment
from members. Furthermore, despite growing evidence about their flexibility and trading success co-operatives are still generally considered
by financial institutions to represent a higher risk than conventional
businesses. Many bank managers remain largely ignorant about them, and
their lack of experience with them makes them cautious and suspicious.
Nevertheless Chaplin and Cowe (1977) found four years ago that the
sources of finance for co-operatives are much the same as for conventional businesses. This proportion is very likely to have increased
since as banks have become more attuned to funding start-ups of all
kinds. A significant reassurance has arrived with the introduction of
the Government Loan Guarantee Scheme. This can be particularly suitable
for co-operatives with their typically low initial capital resources.

Work Satisfaction

Much of the early work at the Open University's Co-operative Research
Unit focussed on the issue of work satisfaction. They found that satisfaction is no higher in co-operatives than in conventional businesses.
However this disguises a number of other simultaneous trends. The co-
operative framework can be an extremely powerful stimulus to employee
involvement in company affairs. This involvement can result in rapid
learning and can profoundly affect the attitudes of those concerned.
Disillusionment and cynicism can arise when expectations are unfulfilled.
But at the other extreme

> 'participation in a co-operative adds a completely new
> dimension to the working lives of some members, even making
> them, according to one member of a co-operative, quite

unsuitable for conventional employment' (Beishon et al. 1978).

Apparent job satisfaction in co-operatives is no higher because, although gaining more from their company, most workers also expect more just because it is a co-operative. These conclusions are similar to those derived from the research evidence on twenty self-managed companies in Yugoslavia reviewed by Garson (1974). Yugoslav workers feel that they should have more influence than they do. Nevertheless few of them want to return to previous systems. Self-management does not actually lead to discontent but does lead to politicisation. Those who participate more desire to participate more. The more democratic the perceived influence structure, the more democratic the desired influence structure.

Co-operative Objectives

A great many co-operatives espouse a multiplicity of objectives. Quite apart from the apparently obvious one of organisational survival (not, incidentally, accepted as obvious by every co-operative) many are created to produce more satisfying work, provide a particular service to the public, demonstrate certain values about political or business organisation, and/or keep certain individuals in jobs. Almost inevitably this leads to some kind of crisis within the first two years when members realise that they can't achieve them all.

The Open University Job Satisfaction Research Programme team outlined the mechanism (Beishon et. al, 1978: 7). In general, employee expectations are raised over a wide range of concerns. Raised expectations may generate confusions over the co-operative's objectives. They may be contradictory, they may be difficult to define or measure, they may be difficult to achieve. In any event establishing concensus may be problematic. Non-agreement or non-achievement in the face of high expectations makes disillusionment virtually inevitable. In particular, employees' raised expectations of influence may require significant organisational innovations, which may be difficult to conceive or implement. As Rosemary Rhoades concluded from her study of Milkwood Co-operative Ltd. (Rhoades, 1980) having too many objectives will result in none being achieved.

Many people assume, particularly those adopting the unitary perspective of industrial relations, that because workers accept the legitimacy of management in co-operatives more readily than in conventional business- es the task of management will be easier. This is not necessarily the case. Co-operatives highlight the changes occurring in the position of management which, until very recently anyway, were being witnessed in all businesses generally. The management prerogative has been modified from the authority of position to the authority of competence and skill. The co-operative framework in addition puts heavy pressure on the way managers perform their role. It requires that they operate with an open and participatory style. Both these changes can make management in a co-operative quite difficult. Certainly research has not found that leadership is a redundant concept in co-operatives. If anything leaders are at least as important as in conventional businesses.

In many cases the leaders who play a major part in creating the co- operative, whether as entrepreneurs, management benefactors or as union fighters against the old employers, find it difficult to maintain their role as effective leaders once the co-operative has started. It takes a different style to run a co-operative than it does to start one. This is least likely to be the case among the smaller alternative co- operatives although in these enterprises too leaders do very frequently emerge and sometimes run into serious problems of relationships with others. One of the fundamental rules promulgated by Roger Sawtell, ex- ICOF Chairman, ICOM and CDA Board member, is that the person leading the set up of the co-operative should leave within five years.

The example of KME perhaps illustrates the dilemma as sharply as any other. The co-operative's creation owed much to the leadership qualit- ies of the two Director Convenors, their ability to negotiate with management and to be credible representatives to the outside world, their command of general meetings and their ability to wield total sol- idarity of the workforce behind them. The same qualities become dysfunctional in a co-operative once it begins trading. Dissent or criticism needs space for expression as part of the dialectic of policy formation- solidarity is no longer as crucial as a relationship of trust which allows all who are interested freely to debate and explore

the alternative possibilities; the command of mass meetings becomes a
somewhat redundant ability when general meetings are no longer sufficient as the primary decision-making locus of a company; and the solidarity built up during a previous failure may present a barrier to
the subsequent diffusion of power.   The KME Director Convenors found
themselves trapped by their historical roles. The fiercer the fight to
survive, the deeper the trap.

Tony Eccles (Purcell and Smith, 1979) derives a handful of other conclusions from the experience of KME. While doubtless clearest in a
'defensive' co-operative of such size the same issues can be traced in
some other co-operatives. Managers may find it difficult to provide
effective organisation unless the co-operative is dependent on them
since the workforce doesn't initially value managerial traits. (This
is less the case in handover co-operatives where sometimes the enthus-
iasm of workers for a share in the control is less than that of the
managers who are offering it.)   Co-operatives may find it difficult to
judge good management and advice from bad, lacking experience, good
information and perhaps good advice. Finally, a distaste for managers,
and/or an unwillingness to pay the market rate for them, may lead co-
operatives to have too few.

Decision-making

> 'The fact that ownership has been democratised does not
> ensure that the government of the enterprise has been
> similarly democratised.... The workers' influence over
> events may become more tenuous in a co-operative than
> in a traditional firm having strong union collective
> bargaining representation' (Eccles, 1979)

The duality of power between workers and traditional management doesn't
disappear in the larger co-operatives but is internalised, with difficulty, among the individuals who are the representatives of both.

Decision-making has attracted perhaps the most interest of co-operative researchers in the UK in recent years although the number of firm
conclusions produced as a result remain very small. A lot has been
done in Yugoslavia. There Garson (1974) has found that, although
managers and experts dominate, workers councils do make a significant

number of proposals on each of the most crucial areas of strategic decision-making (economic problems related to the market, economic problems in co-operating with other companies, internal economic arrangements of the enterprise), and a disproportionate number of these were accepted. A disproportionately small number of workers' proposals were accepted on wages and income, the area most likely to lead to conflict between management and workers.

In this country a detailed study of eighteen areas of decision-making in an East Midlands co-operative revealed an interesting conclusion (private Open University Co-operatives Research United report). The researchers had been called in because the atmosphere in the co-operative had degenerated since its start, people were no longer 'pulling together'. There was a resentment or disaffection with the manager who couldn't understand why. We discovered that in every area of decision-making the members basically agreed with the decisions which had been taken. What frustrated them was that nevertheless they had not been given enough opportunity to share in taking them. Part of the problem was that certain mechanisms or meetings which could have been employed for sounding out opinions or reaching decisions were not being so. The co-operative had kept to its original structure of meetings although this did not always meet the organisation's subsequent decision-making needs. The research team also found that the decisions on which the workers were most content to relinquish their own prerogative were precisely those affecting the structure of meetings and conduct of the co-operative; for example whether or not to have a full time Commonwealth Secretary, whether or not to call in the research team, when and what occurs in General Meetings. Our conclusion was that this carried a risk, for ultimately this area is the base of all decision-making. Who decides who will decide what?

In many ways decisions in co-operatives are similar to those in conventional businesses; they are only as good as they are effectively implemented. Effective implementation invariably means that the decision or policy is both understood and accepted by others involved, otherwise it will be unwittingly obstructed or deliberately sabotaged. To achieve this most companies are moving towards more participatory decision-making procedures. Not all decisions have to handled the same way. Although an obvious point, and one taken for granted in conventional companies, many people unreasonably expect it not to be the case in co-operatives.

The Open University's Co-operative Research Unit has developed a model for analysing decisions to be taken in co-operatives (Thomas and Cornforth, 1980). It begins with understanding of the various processes available for making decisions e.g. the manager or someone else decides autonomously, or after consultation; joint decision-making with both management and workers having the power of veto; majority decision-making; decision by concensus, and so on. In any organisation there are additionally a number of mechanisms that can be used and within which any of those processes can be employed - ordinary general meetings, extraordinary general meetings, ad hoc meetings, standing specialist committees, ad hoc committees, delegations of individuals, and so on. Bearing in mind the particular circumstances and attitudes of people in any organisation it is often relatively easy to reach agreement on how ideally each issue should be dealt with, employing five basic criteria:

  a) is the issue complex?
  b) is it urgent?
  c) is it of long term importance to the future of the co-operative?
  d) is it something all or some of the members are interested in?
  e) does it affect people directly; if so, who?

Often people starting co-operatives hope that issues, and decision-making as an issue, can be resolved informally by relying on members' basic common interests and goodwill. Almost invariably, especially as the co-operative grows, these informal processes degenerate unless built into the co-operative's structure somehow. As Tony Eccles puts it:

  'It isn't that one structural form is best, but that, for
  a given circumstance, some structures are systematically
  and demonstrably better than others' (1981: 397)

Whether or not professional managers are employed, and whatever are the organisation's goals, power and accountability need to be delineated if the organisation is to be effective. Co-operation doesn't mean conflict is avoidable or unnecessary but it should mean eliminating 'unnecessary' conflict caused by poor communication, unclear procedures and so on, so that the co-operative decision-making process can concentrate on issues of genuine disagreement or conflict.

Unions

The unions on the whole have been politely sympathetic to co-operatives in word but, with the exception of a few individual officials and stewards, unhelpful in deed. They remain ambivalent for a number of reasons. The work of Beatrice Webb continues to have considerable influence in the labour movement. At the beginning of the century she maintained that truly democratic workers' co-operatives would flounder in the sea of capitalism. If they survived and succeeded it would be at the cost of becoming mini-capitalists themselves and this would hardly be conducive to the construction of a socialist state. In the 1920s some unions had their fingers burnt when they gave financial support to short-lived building guilds. Today they see a co-operative movement confusingly supporting a hotch potch of ideas and philosophies and managing to attract the allegience of all the major political parties simultaneously - the Left as a way of introducing society-wide change, the Liberals as an expression of local emancipation, the Con-servatives as a way of encouraging workers to accept the 'realities' of survival in a market economy. Neither of the last two are close to the traditional thinking of unions. Many individual co-operative leaders, and others writing in support of co-operatives (notably Peter Jay) (1977) promote them deliberately as a way of reducing or eliminating union power and many co-operatives, as we have seen, flout some of the conditions (pay, working environment) that unions have fought for ever since they existed.

Shop stewards are on the whole suspicious of co-operatives. When they have found themselves working in one, such as KME, they have found the experience stressful and confusing, not sure whether to accept part of the responsibility for management or to maintain their traditional role as adversary against their own elected leaders. According to Peter Smith (1981) full time officials on the whole are a little more sympathetic. They can see how co-operatives could be slotted in along-side major private and public producers as part of the planning agree-ments involved in an investment led reflation, but they do not consider co-operatives to be very important. They will only be suitable for relatively few workplaces and therefore do not offer a solution to the economy-wide problems of the trade union movement.

Eccles offers a challenge in the reverse direction. The common cause between co-operators in a given enterprise suggests the need for union integration, not the multiplicity of occupational unions which presently exists. Reorganising unions to cope would involve greater sophistication and complexity, and would make them more difficult to control. Like any power holders the unions are reluctant to co-operate in the erosion of their own power.

> 'Unions will express polite support whilst remaining
> operationally opposed to co-operatives unless a
> structure can be found which maintains union legitimacy.'
> (Eccles, 1981: 400)

CONCLUSIONS

The co-operative movement in this country, despite the fashionable attention recently afforded it, has not make much significant contribution to employment in the last decade. However, excluding the three Benn enterprises, co-operatives receive less than half the average State financial support per job that is provided for the capitalist sectors. Furthermore the co-operative boom over the last five years has undoubtedly ushered in many vigorously successful co-operatives which will provide much increased employment in the next decade. What might happen, however, is that the spurt in new registrations will gradually fizzle out after five years or so, leaving the sector with, as before, a large number of co-operatives all of the same age.

Whether this happens or not, and how significant co-operatives will feature in the discussions about future industrial organisation, will depend on the philosophical and political perspectives and perceptions of the movement. The 'alternative' co-operatives are an expression of rejection of traditional politics, and of traditional industry and commerce. The larger and more conventional co-operatives are likely to be treated more seriously by the major institutions in our economic industrial society. However they do so at the risk of becoming indistinguishable from any other form of enterprise. If this occurs the point of creating co-operatives at all will be lost. Without some collective and cohering philosophy the sector is unlikely to expand.

At the moment there appear to be two choices on offer for that philosophy - the Christian socialist model, and the labour class struggle model.   The former seems the less likely to attract mass support.   The latter seems unlikely at all given the implications of recent experience.

> 'Worker co-operatives may pose more of a challenge to
> Marxist analysis than capitalism' (Eccles, 1981:   363)

Consequently worker co-operatives in Britain are unlikely to work in great numbers unless worker attitudes and union policies also change.

Whatever happens on the grand canvas the learning experience of working co-operatively is accumulating fast.   There are now too many examples of stressful participation for us to believe that just providing the opportunity is enough.   Like marriage, co-operatives have to be worked at.   It takes time for all involved to learn the skills and adjust to the roles needed for them to run their own business both democratically and effectively.   One of the main conclusions from the Open University's Job Satisfaction Research Programme was framed as follows:

> 'To the extent that it disturbs conventional assumptions
> on the part of both managers and employees, a co-operative
> stimulates attempts at tackling them.   However, the
> difficulties and pitfalls are as clear as the potential
> gains' (Beishon et al: 9).

REFERENCES

Aston, B., Unpublished MA Dissertation 1980, Department of Industrial Relations, University of Warwick.

Beishon, J., Lockett, M., Paton, R., *Job Satisfaction Research Programme: Summary Report on the Open University Project* ,Milton Keynes, Open University Systems Group, 1978.

Campbell, A., Keen, C., Norman, G. and Oakeshott, R., *Worker Owners: The Mondragon Achievement* , London Anglo-German Foundation, 1977.

Chaplin, P. and Cowe, R., *A Survey of Contemporary British Worker Co-operatives* , Manchester Business School Working Paper No.36, 1977.

Cole, G.D.H., *A Century of Co-operation* , Manchester, Co-operative Union, 1945.

Co-operative Development Agency, *Co-ops: A Directory of Industrial and Service Co-operatives* , London, Autumn 1980.

Eccles, T., Workers Co-operatives: The Case of KME. The Limits of Control in John Purcell and Robert Smith (eds.), *The Control of Work*, Macmillan, 1979.

Eccles, T., *Under New Management*, London, Pan 1981.

Garson, G.D., *On Democratic Administration and Socialist Self-Management: A Comparative Survey Emphasising the Yugoslav Experience*, Beverley Hills, Administrative and Policy Study Series: Sage Publications, No. 03-015, Vol.2, 1974.

Industrial Common Ownership Movement, *Directory of Common Ownership Enterprises*, Leeds, 1980.

In the Making: A Directory of Radical Co-operation (published annually with supplement) Sutton, Surrey.

Jay, P., *The Workers Co-operative Economy*, Manchester Statistical Society, 1977.

Jones, D., *British Producer Co-operatives*, in Ken Coates (ed.) The New Worker Co-operatives , Nottingham, Spokesman, 1976.

London Industrial Common Ownership Movement, *Use Your Local Co-operative: The Directory of Co-op Firms in London 1981*, 1981.

Rhoades, R., *Milkwood Co-operative Ltd.*, Milton Keynes, Open University Case Study Series, No.4, 1980.

Scott, Dr. M.G., *Mythology and Misplaced Pessimism: A Look at the Failure Record of New Small Businesses*, paper presented at the United Kingdom Small Business Management Teachers Association. Manchester Business School, 1980.

Smith, P., *Current Trade Union Attitudes to Producer Co-operatives*, presented at Plunkett Foundation's Sixth Co-operative Seminar, Oxford, April 1981.

Thomas, A., with Cornforth, C., A Model of Decision-Making for Worker Co-operatives, in *Fifth Co-operative Seminar, Hertford College, Oxford, 9th-11th April 1980: Papers'*, Oxford, Plunkett Foundation, 1980.

Thornley, J., *Workers Co-operatives: Jobs and Dreams*, London, Heinemann, 1981.

Training and Advisory Services for the Small Retail Business — The Case for Government Action
DAVID KIRBY

In the two research reports on retailing commissioned by the Bolton
Committee (Hall, 1971; Smith, 1971) considerable emphasis was placed
on the need for training and advisory services specifically orientated
to the needs of the smaller business[1]. To 'emphasise the techniques
and problems of small scale retailing and deal with entry problems',
Smith (1971 : 37) advocated the establishment of a national training
scheme, possibly under the auspices of the Economic Development Committee for the Distributive Trades. If coupled with a licensing requirement, such training would raise the low standards of this sector
of the economy, Smith argued, and 'could well succeed in the twin,
highly desirable, objectives of deterring marginal entrants and improving the efficiency and survival chances of those who do open shops'
(Smith, 1971: 36). In the companion report, Margaret Hall (1971: 51)
advocated the establishment of a small central agency not only 'to make
known to traders what services are available to them and to show small
businesses how to make use of them' but also to 'offer consultancy services for a small charge where no existing body can be induced to do so'
(Hall, 1971: 57).

Despite the force of their arguments and the general recognition of
the importance of training and consultancy, no such agencies have been
provided in Britain over the past decade. Admittedly small retail operators can, like the proprietors of any other small business unit,
take advantage of the information and counselling services of the small
firms advisory bureaux set up as a result of the Bolton Committee's recommendations. However, these are orientated more to the needs and
requirements of production industry and few of the queries received at
each centre are from retailers or prospective retailers. To a certain
extent, the Unit for Retail Planning Ltd. might be perceived as fulfill-

ing the recommendation for a specialist information/consultancy service for retailing. Established in 1975 with financial sponsorship from the Departments of the Environment and Transport, the unit is now a private, self-financing enterprise. Inevitably, its activities have tended to reflect the interests of its sponsors which, in the main, have been the large retail organisations and major planning authorities. As a consequence, the unit specialises in neither the needs and requirements of small businesses nor in the methods of retail management, concentrating more on questions related to retail location.

So it would appear that, in the decade since the Bolton Report, the position with regard to small retail businesses has not improved. Indeed, the situation could be said to have worsened and that the need for a training and advisory service is, perhaps, greater now than it was in 1971.

THE NEED FOR RETAIL TRAINING AND ADVISORY SERVICES

Adequacy of Existing Provision

Increasingly the trend in retailing has been towards greater productivity and efficiency and there has been a growing awareness, as in other sectors of the economy, of the need for management training and for sound, reliable information for decision making purposes. Very largely these services are available only to the larger retail organisations, through their own training and research departments or their ability to buy in expertise. As a consequence, many of the services that are provided commercially are orientated, as they were in 1971, to the needs and requirements of the large firm.

In its review of training under the 1964 Industrial Training Act, the Bolton Committee concluded that the machinery set up under the Act was 'inappropriate to the needs of most small firms' (Bolton, 1971: 350) and recommended that small firms should be exempted from the levy/grant system. As a result of subsequent revisions, retail businesses with fewer than ten staff or an annual payroll of less than £30,000 were exempt. As the various surveys (Bates, 1976; Dawson and Kirby, 1979) have revealed, most independent small businesses are considerably smaller than this. Indeed, few employ any staff other than family

members or casual helpers.   Thus it would seem that most independent
small traders are now exempt from levy payments.   However, in the distribution industry at least, the inappropriateness of the machinery remains in that the training initiatives implemented by the Board are orientated more to the needs and requirements of the larger business -
being intended to stimulate the training of staff rather than the training of proprietors.   While much of the material produced by the Board
might be of value to the independent trader, it is not directed at him
and most small, independent retail businesses know very little about
the work of the Board and see little of relevance in the training initiatives it takes.   Even so, the decision in 1981 to disband the Distributive Industry Training Board means that the industry has been deprived of one of the major potential vehicles for initiating training
in this sector of the retail trades (Dawson and Kirby, 1979).

Courses specifically for the independent retailer are offered three
times a year by the College for the Distributive Trades in London
(Richmond, 1981).   These are three day residential courses which can be
run as three one day units.   They cover such topics as:

  a) legal aspects relevant to the independent retailer, staff
     management and motivation.
  b) financial control, including techniques of budgeting and
     cash control, management ratio analysis and financial
     stock keeping.
  c) merchandising techniques and items such as stock selection,
     stock control and pricing.

While relevant to the needs of most small retail businesses, knowledge
of the courses does not appear to be widespread throughout this sector.
Also, it is inevitable that many prospective participants from outside
of the south east are deterred by a London location.

In the grocery trades, at least, training courses are provided by the
various trading organisations.   The Institute of Grocery Distribution,
for instance, offers two different types of course:

  a) short courses introducing the grocery industry and aimed
     mainly at trainees or young managers in multiple organisations.
  b) correspondence courses which cover a much wider spectrum
     of interest, but which, fundamentally, are aimed at the

113

employees of the larger retail organisations. Three
courses are offered. The first is an introductory
course intended 'for young people who have just started
work in retailing. It aims to explain how business
works and how their company is part of a vital industry....
the course supplements a company induction programme'.
The second, leading to the award of an Advanced Certificate, is intended for people who 'wish to develop their
careers' while the third, leading to a Certificate in
Management Studies directed at 'managers and potential
managers'.

Thus, it would seem that these courses are not orientated specifically
to the needs of the owner-manager, and though there is probably much of
value for the small trader within each course, it is unlikely that this
will be recognised fully by potential candidates. Finally, it is doubtful whether distance learning is the most suitable mode of training for
the over-worked, non-academic small trader. As recent surveys have re-
revealed, most traders left school at or before the age of sixteen and
have not received any post-school education (Dawson and Kirby, 1979;
Kirby, 1978). For them, a formal academic correspondence course would
be a most daunting experience and one which even the most highly motiv-
ated would have difficulty completing.

Perhaps of more direct relevance to the small independent food trader
are the training and advisory services offered by the various voluntary
group organisations (Spar, Mace, V.G., etc.). Two types of training
and advisory service are provided. The first, operated by groups such
as V.G., involves no formal training. New entrants are sent to another
store in the group where they receive 'appreciation training'. Once
in business, the group provides advice on various aspects of store management through their store development staff attached to each member
wholesaler. Frequently, centralised courses are offered on specific
topics affecting all traders (such as VAT, metrication, etc.) and, once
again, these are organised by the member wholesaler. For their success,
therefore, the training and advisory services are dependent on the individual wholesaler and certainly the quality of the service varies from
area to area. Indeed, one of the major complaints by affiliated retailers is that frequently they get little in return for their membership.

The alternative strategy is that adopted by an organisation such as Spar. For the past twenty years, Spar has operated a central training department which currently offers its 3,800 members some sixty different courses. These courses, which are organised nationally at training centres in Bath and Coventry, regionally and in-company, cover a wide range of retail management skills, including merchandising, financial control and the control of specialist departments (e.g. bacon handling, fresh fruit and vegetables, etc.). One of the weaknesses of the scheme, as Hunt (1980: 21) has observed, is that 'the retailers who are most in need of the courses are those who, often, are "too busy" running their businesses to attend'. To counteract this problem, Spar has launched a series of self-contained one day seminars held in local areas. The main problems with these are that:

a) they are held on consecutive days and will not eliminate the objections which Hunt identified, many small traders being reluctant to leave their businesses and families for such a prolonged period.

b) they are essentially commercial courses and many retailers will be unable or unwilling to pay the course fees.

c) they are run primarily by a Voluntary Group for its members, Spar believing that it is 'the Spar members who have been trained, and have implemented that training, who can stand their ground' (Hunt, 1980: 21).

Recently the courses have been opened up to all independent retailers, whether Spar members or not. The main problems here seem to be that:

a) other groups may be suspicious of Spar's motives and may not encourage their members to participate, while many unaffiliated retailers are reluctant to be associated with a group in any way (Livesey and Nagy, 1981).

b) retailers not affiliated to Spar will not benefit from the counselling very necessary to ensure that the training material is properly implemented.

Thus it would seem that within the food trades, Spar has recognised the need for such training and advisory services but whether they can be provided successfully by a commercial organisation associated with a voluntary group is open to debate. Also, such organisations are not characteristic of the retail trades and courses like those which Spar is offering are not common.

From this brief review of the services available, therefore, it can be concluded that management training for the small business in the retail trades is not satisfactory, despite the general improvement in small business management education in the decade since the Bolton Report.

The Characteristics of Small Retail Businesses

Having considered the supply of training and advisory services to small retail businesses, it is necessary to consider the market for these services.

In 1979, there were, in Britain, some 357,100 retail businesses and of these 211,900 (59 per cent) were single outlets with an average turnover of less than £79,000 per annum (Table 1). Most of these stores would be extremely small unprofitable businesses employing few, if any, staff (Bates, 1976; Dawson and Kirby, 1979; Thorpe, 1977) and generating low returns on investment[2]. Equally, most would be run by a proprietor who had received no formal training in retailing and who possessed little knowledge of business management methods. What it is necessary to recognise is that entry into small scale retailing is deceptively easy and, as a consequence, this sector of the economy is characterised by:

a) a large number of entrepreneurs from outside of retailing with no experience even remotely relevant to retailing (Kirby, 1978).

b) a high turnover rate - as Bechhofer et al. (1974: 471) observed in Edinburgh, approximately 20 per cent of the shops 'closed or changed hands at least every six to twelve months'.

c) bankruptcy and a high failure rate (Donleavy, 1980) - retailing remains 'one of the easiest ways of losing the savings of a lifetime' (Lewis, 1945: 231).

Indeed, small businesses remain a feature of the British retail system only because:

a) there is 'no lack of individuals prepared to risk their capital in return for the envisaged freedom of running their own business' (Bechhofer and Elliott, 1968: 185).

116

TABLE 1

RETAIL TRADES BY FORM OF ORGANISATION, 1979

	Number ('000)	Average Turnover per Outlet (£'000)
Single Outlets	211.9	78.6
Small Multiples	69.9	106.5
Large Multiples	75.3	374.1
Total	357.1	146.4

Source: Economist Intelligence Unit, 1981.

   b) many businesses are only viable as a result of the
      proprietors working extremely long hours and/or relying
      upon family labour. In many instances the business
      is not the sole source of income, additional revenue
      coming from alternative employment and/or retirement
      or disability pensions.

Given the low levels of expertise characteristic of this sector, it
would seem that there is a potential market for training and advisory
services. However, it is unlikely that the need is recognised by the
traders themselves. Like entrepreneurs in other sectors, many retailers
are not acquainted fully with the problems of this type of business
(Clarke, 1972) and are unaware of how little they know.   Equally, like
most prospective bankrupts, many distrust professional advisers
(Donleavy, 1980). Thus, although there exists a need for such services,
it is unlikely that there exists a demonstrable demand. Rather, the
demand is for the relief of the more immediate, external problems facing
the small trader - the reduction of competition, rents, rates, bureaucracy, etc. (Kirby and Law, 1981). This would suggest that if such
services are to be provided the demand would probably have to be generated by extensive advertising and by packaging the services attractively.

The Need for Small Shops

One of the characteristic features of most western style economies, in
recent years, has been the decline in the number of retail outlets and
the tendency for shop units to increase in scale.   In Britain, this

process has been recognised for several decades and currently it would seem to be operating at an accelerated pace. To many, the concomitant changes in the structure of retailing suggest that the small, local store is an anachronism and that such shops have no part in a modern efficient distribution system. While this may be true of the traditional, inefficient small shop and further closures of such businesses can be expected (particularly in areas of over-provision) there is evidence to suggest that a need for local shops does exist and that the efficient small store will fulfil an important social and economic function in future distribution systems.

In America, for instance, the retail system appears to be polarising. Relatively small convenience stores are being developed to satisfy the need for local shops consequent upon the increasing scale of retail development and the virtual disappearance of the more traditional 'mom and pop' stores (Kirby, 1976a). These shops are used by the majority of consumers for 'topping up', in 'emergencies' and for the purchase of perishables (Kirby, 1976b). Equally, they are used by those consumers, perhaps a minority, unable to travel long distances to shop (for everyday items) or to buy in bulk. As such they complement, rather than compete with, the large store in the retail system.

This trend is being repeated elsewhere in the western world - in Sweden (Lundberg, 1978), in Denmark (Kerndal-Hansen, 1979) and in France, (Litke, 1976). In Britain it is interesting to observe that not only do large shops seem to have relatively little effect on the trade of small shops (Thorpe and McGoldrick, 1974; Thorpe, Shepherd and Bates, 1976) but that one of America's largest convenience store chains ('7-Eleven' owned by the Southland Corporation) has perceived the 'market' for such stores in Britain and recently started trading. So, it would appear that even in the most concentrated and efficient retail systems, there is a need for small, local stores.

In addition, it should be recognised that not all sectors of the community are willing or able to shop at large stores. First, there are those households for whom the trend to mass merchandising is unacceptable. For these, the small, specialist store is important and, with increasing prosperity, it can be expected that the demand for such stores will increase, as Hall (1973) has suggested.

Perhaps of even greater significance are the needs and requirements of the underprivileged sectors of society. Inevitably 'a market system steered by the free choice of consumers alone will tend to favour the bigger and stronger groups of consumers - a development contrary to the superior goal of equality' (Ekhaugen, 1975: 5). With the decline in the number of small, local shops, it is the poor, the aged, the infirm and the immobile which are most disadvantaged. As Daws and Bruce (1971) discovered in Watford, a decline in the provision of local shops would cause hardship to 90 per cent of pensioner households and 70 per cent of the lower socio-economic groups.

Not only does the small local shop provide a social service for the minority of consumers, however, but for the majority also. First, it adds variety to the retail system - variety in both visual terms and in terms of shopping locations and experiences. Second, in both urban and rural environments, the local shop is frequently the focus of community life and point of contact, the shopkeeper acting as a transmitter of information, confidant, social therapist and, often, a social welfare officer caring, particularly, for the wellbeing of the aged and infirm members of the community. In many rural areas there is no alternative to the small shop and its closure quite frequently leads to the breakup of the local community and the further loss of population from the countryside to the town.

Finally, it must be recognised that small shops, like other small firms, 'provide a means of entry into business for new entrepreneurial talent and the seedbed from which new, large companies grow' (Bolton Report, 1971: 343). While this point is recognised in the context of manufacturing, it is often overlooked in the distributive trades, despite numerous examples of its applicability - most notably in Britain by the rise of the giant Tesco empire (Corina, 1971).

From the evidence available, therefore, it would seem that there is a need for small local stores. However, the small shops of the future 'will require a vastly different and more flexible approach than has been manifested so far, and this approach may be beyond the ability of many' (Stacey and Wilson, 1965: 195). If the small trader is unable to adapt to the changing conditions, the only other possibility is to become part of a larger organisation, as Little (1971) has suggested, thereby gaining access to the benefits of large scale buying, mass advertising, management expertise, and central computing facilities which such organisations can provide. This would mean joining a specialist organisation (similar to the American convenience store chains) operating a number of small stores, or a voluntary wholesaling or buying group, similar to those operating in the British grocery trades. However, there are problems with such a solution. First, many small retailers fear the loss of independence which becoming part of a large organisation would involve. Second, such a development results, inevitably, in the loss of many of the advantages of small businesses, particularly their 'special role in innovation and risk taking' (Bolton Report, 1971: 23). Finally, it must be appreciated that, given the profit motive characteristic of such operations, only the more progressive small businesses, and those businesses in the most profitable locations, would be permitted to participate. In all probability, therefore, those stores most in need of aid, and those communities most in need of local shopping facilities, would be deprived of support.

The alternative solution seems to be to help the small retailer to become more viable by extending to this sector of the economy the sort of training and advisory services which are available to big businesses but which, even if they were provided commercially, the small trader would be unable to afford.

THE PROVISION OF TRAINING AND ADVISORY SERVICES

In her report to the Bolton Committee, Margaret Hall made the point, when considering the question of training and advisory services, that 'it is useful to cite foreign experience' (1971: 52). Indeed, several European countries have recognised the need for such services and a broad range of schemes has been provided in many countries for several years. These include training programmes intended to meet the needs of both established firms and new ventures and consultancy and advisory services to aid retailers:
  a) implement their training.
  b) resolve the specific problems facing their particular business.
  c) make more informed decisions.
Quite frequently the training programmes are linked, as in Italy, to a licensing requirement. Here, the freedom to operate a business is

governed by Law No. 426 of 11 June 1971, which has stringent provisions
regarding the registration of businesses, the right to work in distribution and the quantity of retailing.   Under the law, entry is restricted to those who have passed a proficiency test, or have worked in the
business for at least two years or have attended a professional business course recognised by the State.   Clearly such legislation acts not
only as 'a means of restricting entry to the retailing sector, but as a
screening process, deterring those entrants whose chances of survival
are not good, and improving the prospects of those determined to go
ahead' (Smith, 1971: 37).   Traditionally, however, the distributive
trades have been dominated by the philosophy that freedom of entry is
'the most important check on the abuse of market power' (McClelland,
1969: 12) and several countries have abandoned their training requirement.   One such country is Germany where, under the law of 5 August
1957, anyone wishing to operate a retail business had to obtain a
licence which was granted only to persons providing evidence of expertise and good character.   Since 1972, the expertise requirement has
been ruled to be unconstitutional and is now required only for the dispensing of medicines.   In the Netherlands, complex entry regulations
have similarly been relaxed but a proficiency certificate is still required for any retail undertaking, though only one licence for each
business and only the person in charge of the business has to prove
evidence of proficiency.

Despite the relaxation of the licencing arrangement, training programmes are provided in several countries, as are specialist consultancy
and advisory services, often grant aided or heavily subsidised.   Under
the technical services law of 21 March 1973, small businesses in Denmark,
for instance, can obtain a subsidy of approximately 50 per cent of a
consultant's fee and travelling expenses, while in Germany, state
subsidies for employing a consultant range from 25 to 70 per cent of
the costs involved, according to turnover.   In Norway, grants are given
to enable small shops in rural areas to engage a consultant, while state
consultants are employed in the most remote, northern areas where the
problem of shop closure is most acute (Kirby et al., 1981).

In addition to providing financial aid for consultancy, certain
countries have established research and advisory centres specialising
in the problems of small and medium sized businesses.   This is the

case in Holland, where the Economic Institute for Small and Medium
Sized Firms (EIM) and the Central Institute for Small and Medium Sized
Firms (CIMK) are particularly important and have a tradition for work
in retailing.   In Belgium, the business advisory service of the
Economic and Social Institute for Small and Medium Sized Firms provides
small traders with various forms of technical assistance, a similar
function being performed in Luxembourg by the technical assistance department of the Chamber of Commerce.   In Britain, similar services are
provided for large retail organisations (through bodies like the Unit
for Retail Planning Information) and for small industrial concerns
through the small business units of the country's higher educational
establishments and such governmental organisations as The Highlands and
Islands Development Board, The Development Board for Rural Wales, the
Welsh Development Agency, the Council for Small Industry in Rural Areas,
etc.   While these bodies are not precluded from aiding small scale
retailing, there is no tradition for the provision of such a service.

CONCLUSION

Since the Bolton Report of 1971, the arguments for training and advisory
services for small scale retailing have not changed.   However, as a
result of developments since that date, they have, if anything, been
strengthened.   First, the greater emphasis in retailing on management
training and research has meant that the gap has widened between those
(large) retail businesses with the ability to pay for such services and
those without.   Inevitably these have been the smallest, least profitable concerns.   Equally, the emphasis on manufacturing industry in the
various small business management courses which have emerged since 1971
has produced an imbalance between small production industries and small
businesses in the service trades.   At the same time, the decade since
Bolton has witnessed the continued decline of the small retail business,
possibly at an accelerated pace, and the realisation that such businesses play an important social and economic function in contemporary
society.

If the small retail business is to continue to fulfil this function,
the management gap between large and small retail firms needs to be
reduced.   Since the publication of the Bolton Committee Report in 1971,
this seems to have been widened rather than reduced and it can be argued

that if any progress is to be made in this direction, there is a need for an independent service provided, or subsidised, by Government.

When considering the question of subsidised services, the Bolton Committee identified four criteria which, they felt, should be satisfied. These were:

a) that the service is needed.

b) that private enterprise cannot or will not provide it.

c) that the economic benefit to the nation deriving from the services is greater than the cost.

d) that users of the services cannot or should not be expected to pay their full cost.

In the preceding discussion, the case for management advisory services for small retail businesses has been made and experience over the past ten years has demonstrated that these services have not been provided, satisfactorily, by private enterprise. However, even if they had been provided, it is doubtful whether those businesses most in need would have availed themselves of the service or would have been able or willing to pay the full cost. Indeed, this is probably one of the major reasons why such services have not been provided extensively on a commercial basis to date. This being the case, it is only the cost benefit criterion which remains unanswered and without detailed analysis, it is difficult to determine whether the economic benefit to the nation would outweigh the cost of provision. Certainly savings can be achieved through the creation of a more efficient retail system and there could be economic benefits to both the consumer (in the form of lower prices) and the entrepreneur (in the form of greater security and higher returns on investment). However, perhaps the main economic argument for subsidising such a service is the fact that without an efficient commercial service infrastructure, the effectiveness of development aid to both rural areas and the inner cities is reduced considerably. This has been recognised in Scandinavia (Kirby et. al, 1981) and the Development Board for Rural Wales has embarked upon a programme intended to strengthen the infrastructure of rural Wales, believing that a sound infrastructure is as important to the economy as is the stimulation of production and the creation of job opportunities.

As part of this programme, the Board, in collaboration with the author, has launched a training and advisory programme for village shop-

123

keepers. The programme, which is intended to help shopkeepers help themselves, is divided into three sections:

a) A formal training programme, the purpose of which is to introduce the participants to basic elements of modern retail management and to encourage the participants to reappraise their own business operations. The course is divided into four modules (covering Stock Management, Financial Management, Instore Management and Customer Management). Each module lasts for a day and an evening and each is separated by a period of 4-6 weeks to ensure that the proprietor is not away from his business for a prolonged period and to allow for implementation.

b) A forum for discussion where participants can not only discuss the course and ensure understanding, but can consider common problems and try to identify solutions, possibly utilising the resources of the Board and/or involving group action.

c) An advisory service consisting of on-site visits by a consultant to ensure that the techniques are properly understood and implemented and to advise on specific problems relating to the particular business.

While it is too early to comment on the success of the programme, initial results are encouraging and the experiment is being monitored by the EEC Social Fund with a view to implementing similar programmes in other areas. Certainly the problems facing small scale retailing are not unique to rural Wales and it would seem that, as in 1971, 'a general improvement in the performance of small traders.....is necessary if they are to play successfully their future role' (Smith, 1971: 37). If this improvement is to be achieved, government backed training and advisory services seem essential, as Hall and Smith recognised in 1971.

ACKNOWLEDGEMENT

The research on which this paper is based was funded by the Leverhulme Trust Fund and the author is grateful to his assistant on this project, Mr. Martin Day, who was responsible for the initial review of existing provisions.

NOTES

[1.] A small business in the retail trades is presently regarded as one
with a turnover of £200,000 per annum or less (See Wilson, 1979).

[2.] In 1979, the average single outlet employed 4.3 persons and had a
gross margin of 26.4 per cent (£20,750).   By comparison a branch
of a large multiple would employ sixteen persons and generate a
gross margin of 28.7 per cent (£107,367).

REFERENCES

Bates, P., *The Independent Grocery Retailer: Characteristics and
Problems - a Report of a Survey,* Research Report No.23 Retail Outlets
Research Unit, Manchester Business School, 1976.

Bechhofer, F., Elliott, B., An approach to a study of small shopkeepers
and the class structure, *European Journal of Sociology,* Vol.9,
pp. 180-202, 1968.

Bechhofer, F., Elliott, B., Rushforth, M. and Bland, R., Small Shopkeepers: matters of money and meaning, *The Sociological Review,* Vol.
22, No.4, pp. 465-480, November 1974.

Bolton, J.E., Small Firms: *Report of the Committee of Inquiry on Small
Firms.* HMSO. 1971.

Clarke. P.. *Small Businesses: how they survive and succeed.* David and
Charles. 1972.

Corina. M.. *Pile it high and sell it cheap.   The authorised biography
of Sir John Cohen,* Weidenfield and Nicholson, 1971.

Daws, L.F. & Bruce, A.J., *Shopping in Watford,* Building Research Station,
1971.

Dawson, J.A. and Kirby, D.A., *Small Scale Retailing in the UK.,* Saxon
House, 1979.

Donleavy, D., Causes of bankruptcy in England, in Gibb A. and Webb, T.,
Policy Issues in Small Business Research, Saxon House, 1980.

Economist Intelligence Unit Annual Review of Retailing, *Retail Business,*
Part 278, pp. 3-13, April 1981.

Ekhaugen, K., *Implications of the movement towards concentration,* paper
presented at the 22nd International Study Conference at Gottlieb
Duttweiler Institut fur wirtschaftliche und Soziale Studien, Zurich,
1975.

*Financing of Small Firms (The), Interim Report of the Committee to Review
the Functional of Financial Institutions,* Cmnd.7503, London, HMSO,
1979 (The Wilson Report).

Hall, M., *The small unit in the Distributive Trades*, Research Report No.8, Committee of Inquiry on Small Firms, HMSO, 1971.

Hall, M., The prospects for small shopkeepers, *Retail and Distribution Management*, pp. 28–30, July–August 1973.

Hunt, B., Briefing the front-line troops: How Spar trains its independent grocers, *The Training Officer*, pp. 20–21, January 1980.

Kerndal-Hansen, O., Retail Planning in Denmark, in Davies, R. *Retail Planning in the European Community*, Saxon House, 1979.

Kirby, D.A., The North American Convenience Store – implications for Britain, in Jones, P. & Oliphant R. (ed.), *Local Shops. Problems and Prospects*, Unit for Retail Planning Ltd., Reading, 1976a.

Kirby, D.A., The Convenience Store phenomenon: the rebirth of America's small shop, *Retail and Distribution Management*, Vol.4, No.3, pp. 31–33, May–June 1976b.

Kirby, D.A., What happened to the local grocer? *Retail and Distribution Management*, Vol.6, No.5, pp. 52–55, September–October 1978.

Kirby, D.A. and Law, D.C., The birth and death of small retail units in Britain, *Retail and Distribution Management*, Vol.9, No.1, pp. 16–19, January–February 1981.

Kirby, D.A., Sjøholt, P., Stølen, J.A., *The Norwegian Aid Programme to shops in sparsely-populated areas: an assessment of the first four years* (English summary version), Norwegian Fund for Market and Distribution Research, Oslo, 1981.

Lewis, W.A., Competition in Retail Trade, *Economica*, Vol.XII, No.4, pp. 202–234, November 1945.

Litke, B., Renaissance du magasin proximite, *Libre Service Actualite*, No.600, pp. 38–39, 1976.

Little, R.W., The Supra-firm: key to small retailer survival, *University of Washington Business Review*, Vol.30, No.2, pp. 32–47, Winter 1971.

Livesey, F. and Nagy, E.A., Independents versus Affiliation, *Retail and Distribution Management*, Vol.9, No.3, pp. 26–28, May–June 1981.

Lundberg, H.G., *Närköp: local shops*, Co-op document No.5, K.F. International Department, Stockholm, 1978.

McClelland, W.G., The Distributive Sector, *The Three Banks Review*, pp. 3–21, December 1969.

Richmond, N., Courses for the Small Retail Business at CDT, *LRMC News*, Small Business edition, July 1981.

Smith, A.D., *Small Retailers: Prospects and Policies*, Research Report No.15, Committee of Inquiry on Small Firms, HMSO, 1971.

Stacey, N.A.H. & Wilson, A., *The Changing Pattern of Distribution*, Pergamon Press, 1965.

Thorpe, D., *The Independent Toy Retailer. A Study of his characteristics and comments*, Research Report No.28, Retail Outlets Research Unit, Manchester Business School, 1977.

Thorpe, D. & McGoldrick, P.J., *Carrefour: Caerphilly: Consumer reaction*, Report No.12, Retail Outlets Research Unit, Manchester Business School, 1974.

Thorpe, D., Shepherd, P.M. and Bates, P., *Food retailers and Superstore Competition: A Study of Short-term impact in York, Northampton and Cambridge*, Report No.25, Retail Outlets Research Unit, Manchester Business School, 1976.

Wilson, H., *Studies of Small Firms' Financing*, Research Report No.3, HMSO, 1979.

The Female Entrepreneur — American Experience and its Implications for the UK

JEAN WATKINS

Since the publication of the Bolton Report ten years ago the entrepreneurial behaviour of males has been studied extensively.   Attention
has been paid to the characteristics, motivations, problems and management styles of male entrepreneurs, but little interest has so far been
shown in the divergent problems, needs and characteristics of female
entrepreneurs.[1]

If women as a group are judged worthy even of mention within the
small firms context they appear as appendages to a male-led 'family'
business. Their role is an ambivalent one.   Carrying extra responsibilities within the family and thus allowing the male entrepreneur to
concentrate his attentions on business matters, but simultaneously
carrying, particularly in the early years, an often unrewarded and
under-recognised responsibility for the administrative necessities of
business life (Boswell, 1973).   Even when the significance of this
dual role is recognised (Scase and Goffee, 1980) the key question of
succession within the family firm is addressed only in terms of the
needs and abilities of the sons.

To some extent this neglect of the woman as entrepreneur is an arti-
fact, resulting from the concentration of British entrepreneurship/small
business research on the manufacturing sector (perhaps 10 per cent of
all small firms), rather than on research programmes which give weight
to the characteristics and problems of the small firms sector as a
whole. But whatever the reason for the neglect, recent American
research has tried to correct the imbalance by focusing attention specifically on women-led businesses. US research and policy interest is
relatively recent. At the time of Bolton, American interest in the
female entrepreneur was also minimal but it has since expanded considerably;   this paper will attempt to outline and review what has been done

since that time in the USA and examine the questions American experience must raise for the United Kingdom. For, in the USA, not only has
research been undertaken to determine whether the creation and development of businesses may be undertaken for different reasons, and whether
they encounter unique problems, but this research has contributed to
the creation by the federal government and the private sector of special
programmes to encourage women to go into business on their own.

EARLY AMERICAN STUDIES

In 1973 The Centre for Venture Management published the second edition
of its seminal bibliography, 'The Entrepreneur and New Enterprise
Formation: A Resource Guide'. For the first time a separate category
was established for the female entrepreneur. Since the publication of
the first edition in 1970 a small literature had developed. This was
popular and anecdotal rather than research-based, but the editors felt
that:

> 'While the entries in this section are few in number, we
> feel that particular attention should be brought to the
> female entrepreneur, the emerging role of women in business,
> the need for research in the subject of women entrepreneurs
> and most importantly the need for more women to become
> entrepreneurs.' (Schreier and Komives, 1973)

The following year the Centre itself took an initiative to fulfil its
own action programme when Schreier (1975) undertook a pilot research
project to examine the female entrepreneur and determine on the basis of
in-depth interviews what characteristics would best describe her.
Women were interviewed in order that information could be collected on
the following characteristics:

    a) data concerning the business size, type, etc.

    b) starting the business - How? Why?

    c) development of the business.

    d) previous work experience.

    e) experience in starting other businesses.

    f) family background.

    g) schooling.

    h) attitudes towards risk.

    i) perception of the entrepreneur as a female.

j) the women's future plans.

This early research found that the overall picture of the characteristics of male and female entrepreneurs was strikingly similar, particularly in what were felt potentially to be the more critical areas.
These Schreier highlighted as reasons for starting, family history,
risk preferences, marriage and family.

It is easy to understand why, in broad terms, this should be so. The
personal factors traditionally associated with a successful entrepreneurial event - such as high need for achievement, self-confidence,
technical and business prowess, etc. are by no means absent from the
female population. However, they are normally regarded as less positive characteristics in women than in men (i.e. as compromising a
woman's femininity). As such, these traits and accomplishments are
less well-developed among women than men since very different general
social expectations of women and men are inculcated during schooling
and induction into working life. This was perhaps more true during the
40s, 50s and early 60s than of late - but these were the formative
years for the fourteen women in Schreier's sample. What one might
expect would simply be fewer independent businesswomen than independent
businessmen - not people who were necessarily different in kind other
than in gender. However, it was clear that women were tending to open
businesses of a certain (restricted) kind - those embodying typically
'female' occupations (particularly in 'clean' service trades) - rather
than matching the complete profile of male-led businesses.

Schreier's work is inconclusive due to the restricted geographical
coverage and small sample size, although in fairness it should be
added that it was intended simply as a pilot for a national survey
which never came to fruition.[2] However, similar work was carried out
by Schwartz (1976) who investigated a somewhat broader sample in greater
depth. The methodology was more person-centred, and addressed
questions such as:

a) Who is the female entrepreneur? Do women entrepreneurs
   possess characteristics similar to those of male
   entrepreneurs?

b) Why do some women shun the security of more traditional
   paths?

131

c) How do women view themselves in their entrepreneurship
   role?

d) How do women see the attitudes of people who do business
   with or work with them (i.e. banks, investors, customers,
   suppliers)?

e) Can women identify any reasons for success that are
   unique to themselves as women?

f) Can women develop the necessary qualities that are
   considered essential to entrepreneurship?

Most of Schwartz's sample firms again fell within the service category.
The main aim of the study was to develop a better understanding of the
female entrepreneur and thereby help to determine the special education
and training needs of self-employed women and women who would like to
become self-employed. She also found, like Schreier, that female
entrepreneurs highlighted as their major motivations the need to achieve,
the desire to be independent, the need for job satisfaction and economic necessity; and that the responses corresponded closely with the
responses of male entrepreneurs when asked about their major motivations. Interestingly, Schwartz noted that more than half of her respondents had held management - or semi-administrative - positions
before going into business themselves.

Almost all the female entrepreneurs who were questioned felt that
they and other entrepreneurs were 'non-conformers'. They believed that
their success required an aggressive determination to 'make things
happen', and that being an entrepreneur required a certain amount of
toughness. Within the firm this manifested itself in a tendency towards
an autocratic style of management; the female entrepreneurs watched
and controlled their businesses carefully. But it was clear that it
was in relation to dealings outside the firm that these traits were
most important.

Respondents considered that there was financial discrimination against
them during the start-up stage. Many went as far as to say that credit
was denied them just because they were women. In general, putting together the necessary initial capital was the greatest challenge they
had faced in starting and developing the business.

Another significant obstacle was overcoming their lack of training
and business knowledge; they indicated that they had to learn basic

132

skills and behaviour patterns such as:

a) tackling business problems as a leader.

b) wading through confusing details to get to the crux of the business problem.

c) finding ways of compensating for lack of experience:

   (i) from no formal education in school of business and finance.

  (ii) at management levels in the business world itself.

d) dealing with sources of credit and financing.

e) negotiating contracts and dealing with unions.

f) wading through laws and regulations on how business must report its activities.

When asked what they considered to be one of the biggest mistakes they had made, Schwartz found that the majority of female entrepreneurs identified underestimating the cost of operating their business and marketing their product or service.

They felt almost unanimously that women who demonstrate entrepreneurial characteristics and inclinations have a good chance to become as successful entrepreneurs as their male counterparts - once they had overcome the initial problems.

In general, Schwartz's problems are consistent with what is known of achieving women generally and of the problems they face. For example, Henning[3] studied 125 achieving women in Canada and found that they tended to be either only children or the oldest girl in an all girl family, had strong self-esteem and were close to their fathers.

Henning also found that females achieve well during early school years, but their achievement tends to diminish as they reach adolescence and adulthood. Perhaps this is because society has not expected women to succeed (for example, by wielding power in the business world), but to be 'feminine' i.e. submissive, unassertive, emotional and sociable. These expectations can become self-fulfilling prophecies.   To succeed in the business world qualities such as determination, assertiveness and objective and analytical thinking are required whether male or female. In our present context the implication is that large numbers of potentially successful women never consider entrepreneurship as a

career option due to early sexual stereotyping and social conditioning
while in school. The problem is, argues Henning, that a man with these
traits is a 'great guy' while a woman traditionally has been 'unfeminine'. Henning's research is consistent with work recently carried out
in Great Britain in which it was noted that girls did not do as well
educationally in mixed sex secondary schools as in all girls schools,
whereas boys performance showed no marked difference in either
situation.

More recently Hisrich and O'Brien (1981) have sought to extend our
knowledge of the American female entrepreneur through a series of depth
interviews with twenty-one women business founders in the Boston area.
The characteristics and motivations reported tended to confirm the
studies discussed above, but greater attention was paid to the practical
business problems which the women had faced or were facing.

Respondents were asked to rate a number of potential problems on a
five point scale from insignificant to very significant. Almost 45 per
cent of respondents indicated that, in general, bank finance was a
significant problem. More specifically inability to offer adequate
security also came high. Another significant problem area was overcoming society's beliefs that women are not as serious as men about
business.

A few other problems were noted as being significant by some respondents only. These included lack of management experience and lack of
involvement with business colleagues. Hisrich and O'Brien questioned
the causes of variance in the level of significance in these problems.
Is there, they asked, anything in the female entrepreneur's background,
education or type of business that influences the degree of severity
experienced? They found that there was no relationship between the
respondent's educational level or background and the level of significance of the problem. (They felt, however, that this may in part be
explained by the high level of education in the sample.) However, the
nature of the business did   seem important. Those women in architecture, city planning and similar services found most difficulty
obtaining finance. Females in distribution had least problems. Female
entrepreneurs in construction and manufacturing had the most significant
problems in terms of being able to offer adequate security for loans.
Significant problems due to lack of business training were prevalent in

134

service, architecture, planning and computer services.   Female
entrepreneurs in architecture and planning, computer services and construction reported the most significant problems related to overcoming
society's belief that women are not as serious as men about business.

Thus the overall conclusion was that female entrepreneurs do experience varying business problems which reflect the type of business
rather than educational or background characteristics.   Female entrepreneurs in non-traditional areas experienced more significant problems,
particularly in obtaining finance, lack of security and overcoming
society's belief that women are not as serious as men about business.

US GOVERNMENT SUPPORT FOR FEMALE ENTREPRENEURS

In part as a response to research such as that reported above and in
part through the general stimulus to women's affairs through the 1977
International Women's Year (National Commission 1978), US Government
interest in the female entrepreneur has been increasingly aroused from
the mid-70s on.   By 1977 the Small Business Administration felt able
to claim:

'It has conclusively been shown that women business owners
encountered more obstacles and faced more risk financially,
socially, economically, culturally and legally than men
business owners face.'

In response, in August of that year, President Carter established his
Task Force on Women Business Owners.   President Carter's mandate to
this Task Force was as follows:

a) To identify existing data on women entrepreneurs, assess
   their adequacy, identify needs for additional data and
   propose methods of collecting them.

b) To identify the primary practices or conditions which:

   (i)   discourage women from becoming entrepreneurs or,

   (ii)   have the effect of discriminating against women
          entrepreneurs or placing them at a competitive
          disadvantage.

c) To assess current federal programmes and practices which
   have the effect of discriminating against women entrepreneurs or placing them at a competitive disadvantage.

d) Based on these assessments, propose changes in the
   federal law, regulations, and practices for carrying
   out the commitment of the Administration, and advise
   as to the impact, if any, of such changes on the
   federal budget (SBA 1979).

The Task Force found many obstacles facing women entrepreneurs, including a lack of management and technical skills. It concluded that
these deficiencies resulted, in part, from discriminatory practices.
The Task Force also noted, echoing the academic literature, that:
   '..... the similarities between male and female
   entrepreneurs were far greater than their differences'.
while stressing that:
   '..... the major difference exists in the nature and
   extent of barriers placed before them especially when
   considering initial financing'.

One of the major conclusions of the Task Force was that more information was needed as to the size and characteristics of business ownership by women in America:
   'Although the Task Force was able to glean some information
   about women business owners, there is currently little
   reliable data on which to realistically estimate the size
   or characteristics of business ownership by women in
   America. The existing statistical data is out of date,
   and does not capture all the characteristics of the
   owners and their firms. Yet such data is necessary, not
   only to measure the number of female entrepreneurs in
   America but also to design and monitor future programmes.'

It went on to name specific recommendations for further studies,
calling for research directed towards:
   a) Analysing the competencies and skills of business
      owners in the area of capital formation and financing.
   b) Identifying the special problems of women business
      owners in order to give them support and improve
      understanding between men and women in business.
   c) Assessing the types of assistance, information and
      education needed by women who are establishing a
      new business, or maintaining or expanding an existing

one ... namely counselling, advice, publications, lectures, workshops and so forth.

d) Assessing the various programmes now being provided by federal agencies, universities and other organisations for women business owners; analysing those that are most effective, developing model programmes based on these findings; testing them and making necessary modifications; then making them available to women at no cost or for a reasonable fee.

The completion of the work of the Task Force did not mean interest in the female entrepreneurs has flagged. Two developments are particularly noteworthy. First, in 1979 the Department of Commerce agreed that the Census Bureau should update its 1972 survey on women-owned businesses by conducting a special survey of demographic data on women business owners and their enterprises. According to the US Bureau of Labor Statistics:

a) the self-employed woman is likely to be in her mid-forties, white and operating a small service or retail business.

b) she earns less than either self-employed men or salaried women.

c) compared to all large and small US firms the 407,025 women-owned businesses identified represented only 4.6 per cent of all US firms.

d) women-owned businesses were clustered in industries that require low capitalisation and were labour intensive such as services and retail trade. These industries tend to show a lower return on investment.

e) California and New York were the states with the highest percentages of women-owned businesses, and these tended to be located in major cities.

f) only 13 per cent of women-owned businesses had paid employees and, of the employer firms, 73 per cent had fewer than five employees.

The implications of these figures are disturbing in terms of economic and social equity and are discussed briefly below. The important point to note here is that information exists in a form in the US on which policy, and ultimately action, can be based.

The second development is more fundamental in institutional terms. During May 1979 President Carter issued an Executive Order creating a National Women's Business Enterprise Policy and laying down arrangements for the development, co-ordination and implementation of a national programme in support of women's business endeavours (Carter 1979). This mandates the SBA to ensure 'affirmative action' (i.e. positive discrimination) toward women-led businesses in areas as diverse as management training, technical information and procurement assistance. Responsibility for implementing this policy is vested in a separate Office of Women in Business within the SBA (United States Small Business Administration), in the charge of an SBA Deputy Director. It is too early to form an objective view of the impact of this policy initiative, but some indication of the scale of operation is given by figures for attendance at outreach business seminars for women (30,000 within two years), federal contracts awarded to women-led businesses (1980: £15m) and SBA loans (1980: $309m). All these figures are on an upward trend (Kienast and Walter, 1981).

LESSONS FOR THE UNITED KINGDOM

An extensive survey of British small firms literature has failed to uncover any publication of substance dealing specifically with the female entrepreneur. Vis a vis the USA, we are still at the stage of development which the Centre for Venture Management identified in 1973, that of anecdotal literature.

One potentially relevant area of literature about women at work in the United Kingdom concerns the number of women who acquire management and executive positions, their characteristics and problems.

Women in the UK now account for about 41 per cent of the total workforce but only 2 per cent are classed as managers - many more men than women fill positions of responsibility such as bank managers or senior executives in industry. In the professions women are beginning to make some progress but, having started from a very low base line, they are still a tiny minority. This cannot but depress the size of the pool from which potential entrepreneurs are drawn.

One major study is that by Fogarty, Allen and Walters (1981) who looked closely at women in top jobs in Britain from 1968-79.   Here they discussed the position of women in industrial companies examining in particular the number of women who acquire management and executive positions.   However, in America this school of research has been taken a stage further: tentative comparisons of the characteristics of female entrepreneurs and female executives have been made (Sexton and Kent, 1981).

Thus it is clear that Britain is lagging far behind the USA in its knowledge of the female entrepreneur.[4]   This is important since the extent to which findings regarding the American small business sector can act as more than a general model for the United Kingdom is a very open question.   (For example, in the United States there are three times as many independent businesses per head of population as in the United Kingdom.)   We have no real knowledge as to whether similar research on female entrepreneurship carried out here would yield comparable findings to research carried out in the United States.

American experience described above gives a clear indication that the female entrepreneur as an agent in the creation of wealth and employment opportunity (for herself and others) is an underdeveloped human resource within the USA, that this has been recognised and clear action taken.

In particular, positive discrimination is being practised through the SBA to rectify the clearly marginal position in which the Bureau of Labour Statistics data shows that the typical woman in business now finds herself.   The policies being implemented are in many ways analogous to those promoted during the sixties and early seventies to encourage business formation and development by economically and socially marginal ethnic minorities.

Unfortunately, within the British context we are not able to answer basic questions about the scale and diversity of the population of female-led businesses, given the lack of specific published research and the well-known difficulties regarding statistics concerning the small firms sector as a whole.

What is required is research drawing on a number of disciplines to answer basic questions, within the British context such as:

a) the extent and nature of female entrepreneurship
   in Britain.
b) the characteristics and motivations of female
   entrepreneurs.
c) the particular problems she faces in dealing with
   suppliers, customers, bankers and others.
d) the identification of systematic or random biases
   against the female entrepreneur together with
   proposals for their removal.
e) an analysis of the social and economic contribution
   which the female entrepreneur can and could make,
   given limited encouragement.

Certainly the female entrepreneur has been neglected for quite long
enough, even though the general environment for women at work has
improved since the publication of the Bolton Report. As has been
already noted there are now marginally more female executives and
managers. The last ten years have also seen the enactment of the Sex
Discrimination Act in 1975, and the development of limited positive
discrimination operating in favour of women in employment and training.
Women in employment in Britain are increasingly breaking into previously
masculine domains. There are many women now doing jobs in which members
of their sex were not represented in 1975 when the Sex Discrimination
Act was passed.

Indeed, in terms of access to jobs, opportunities are now theoretic-
ally much more equal but they are none the less still unequal in the
demands they make on a boy's/girl's motivation, determination and self-
confidence. To choose surveying, engineering or management traineeship
with one of the multinational companies boys mainly need certain
academic qualifications. Girls need these plus the guts, the self-
confidence to stand out in a crowd, to differ from their peers, to put
up with boring jokes about women's liberation and to be prepared to
answer personal questions about marriage plans at interviews. In other
words, to make what would be a perfectly ordinary choice for an
ordinary boy, a girl has to be a bit extraordinary (Miller,1978). It
is also apparent that once a girl has had the stamina to break through
these barriers her promotion prospects will be nowhere near as good as
her male counterparts - perhaps it is at this time that women could or

140

should branch out on their own to fulfil their own expectations and regain their impaired job satisfaction.

In a period of high (and growing) unemployment and a clear government commitment to encouraging the creation and development of small firms, ignorance about the size, characteristics and potential of that group of businesses run by women, or those that could be run by women, constitutes a surprising and worrying gap in our knowledge. But equally it holds forth the prospect of exciting future challenges both to researchers and policy makers alike.

ACKNOWLEDGEMENT

Research in the New Enterprise Centre on female entrepreneurship is sponsored by the Small Business Unit of Shell U.K. Ltd. This support is gratefully acknowledged.

NOTES

1. A careful reading of the Bolton Report and its principal research reports has failed to identify any instance in which the gender of the small business man was mentioned, let alone raised as an issue requiring discussion of possible differences in business goals, problems or social and economic impact. In the intervening ten years no publication of consequence has appeared in the British literature which has addressed motivation, special circumstances, particular problems or potential impact of the female entrepreneur.

2. The death of its sponsor, Karl Bostrom, meant that the activities of the Centre for Venture Management could only be conducted on a much reduced scale.

3. Quoted by Schwartz (1976).

4. No listings in the current LBS Small Business Bibliography (Dowell 1980–81).

REFERENCES

Boswell, J., *The Rise and Decline of Small Firms*, London, Allen & Unwin, 1973.

Carter, President J., *Executive Order 13138*, The White House, Washington D.C., May 1979.

Fogarty, M. et al., *Women in Top Jobs, 1968-1979*, London, Heinemann Education 1981.

Hisrich, R. and O'Brien, M., 'The Woman Entrepreneur' in Vesper, K.H., (ed.), *Frontiers of Entrepreneurship* Research, Babson Centre for Entrepreneurial Studies, Wellesley, Mass, 1981.

Kienast, K. and Walter, P., *Delphi Study of Economic Factors Contributing to and Inhibiting Success of Women Entrepreneurs*, Conference on Entrepreneurship Research, Babson, Wellesley, Mass, 1981.

Miller, R., *Equal Opportunities - A Career Guide*, Penguin Books Ltd., Harmondsworth, 1978.

National Commission on the Observance of International Women's Year, *The Spirit of Houston: The First National Women's Conference*, Washington D.C., 1978.

S.B.A. (United States Department of Commerce), *Women and the U.S. Small Business Administration*, Washington D.C., July 1979.

Scase, R. and Goffee, R., *The Real World of the Small Business Owner*, London, Croom Helm, 1980.

Schreier, J. and Komives, J., *The Entrepreneur and New Enterprise Formation: a Resource Guide*, Centre for Venture Management, Milwaukee, Wn., 1973.

Schreier, J., *The Female Entrepreneur: A Pilot Study*, Centre for Venture Management, Milwaukee, Wn., 1975.

Schwartz, E.B., 'Entrepreneurship: A New Female Frontier', *Journal of Contemporary Business*, Vol.5, Winter 1976: 47-76.

Sexton, D. and Kent, C., 'Female Executives versus Female Entrepreneurs' in Vesper, K.H., (ed.), *Frontiers of Entrepreneurship Research*, Babson Centre for Entrepreneurial Studies, Wellesley, Mass., 1981.

The Entrepreneurial Base of the Large Manufacturing Company
MICHAEL CROSS

The key objective of the study on which this paper is based was to explore the apparent inverse relationship between the size of a manufacturing company's workforce and the number of its employees leaving to become self-employed (Chinitz, 1961). There were three other objectives:

a) to identify the 'entrepreneurial base' within a large manufacturing company and to describe the personal, social and economic parameters of the individuals who make up this base.

b) to explore ways within the company which might be used to assist these would-be entrepreneurs.

c) to examine the differences between those individuals exhibiting entrepreneurial ambitions and those who exhibit no such inclinations.

METHODOLOGY

In all, four simple criteria were developed as representing the minimum 'description' of an acceptable host-company:

a) the company should be based in the Northern Region, and preferably in the North East, for reasons of logistics.

b) the site at which the work was to be undertaken should be the main production and headquarters site and so include employees of a wide range of skills, occupations and status.

c) there should be no policy of enforced (involuntary) redundancy in operation either at present, or in the recent past.

d) the host-company should give full co-operation and limit

143

the research in as few ways as possible.

In order to collect the necessary data it was felt that, because of the range and complexity of the issues to be covered, personal interviews should be conducted at intervals of at least six months to introduce a longitudinal element into the study. With these few simple criteria and a basic idea of what the data collection exercise would involve, a number of potential host-companies were approached.

After a number of diplomatic refusals, a suitable host-company (a large chemical company in the North East of England) was found and full agreement was reached over how the work should proceed. However, after embarking on the negotiations and implementing the data collection exercise, a number of modifications to the methodology were necessary.

At all times the host-company had the right of veto, and at least the right to question any aspect of the work as it progressed. As the degree of trust and commitment shown by the host-company to the researcher increased (largely by members of the Personnel Department and of the Resettlement Group), so did their willingness to release more information.

Two aspects of the initial relationship with the host-company directly affected the research methodology. First, the preliminary negotiations with the host-company took longer than was anticipated. As a direct consequence of this, it was regarded as important to establish as quickly as possible the personal employment strategies of individual managers. These data were collected by means of a self-completion questionnaire (the 'Resettlement Audit'). The Resettlement Audit design was largely based on methods and questionnaires known to have been successful in similar situations e.g. the Management Development Audit of the TSD and the Job Analysis Methods of HAY-MSL. By means of the Audit, data were collected on:

a) the individuals' personal background and degree of present commitments - FREEDOM TO ACT.

b) their work history and nature of present position - ABILITY TO ACT.

c) and their employment intentions - DIRECTIONS OF INTEREST AND ACTION TAKEN TO DATE.

The Audit was pre-tested and distributed to managers in two stages.

144

Of the 648 managers who had contacted the host-company's Resettlement Group, 444 received copies of the Resettlement Audit and 229 usable replies were received.

Second, the methodology was affected by the action research/process consultation role of the researcher. From the outset of the research, the host-company requested some degree of 'intervention' by the researcher and his colleagues. By explicitly adopting this approach, the researcher was directly affecting the data (in the form of individual managers' attitudes and perceptions towards employment change) to be collected. This situation was unavoidable because by the very act of being allowed into the company to conduct the research the researcher and his colleagues have, individually and collectively, changed the perceptions and attitudes of some members of the host-company. Thus, we were forced (to paraphrase Schein) to think through everything undertaken in terms of its probable impact on the host-company and its members. The Audit was therefore designed to constitute a valid and useful intervention, and to collect the initial data (Schein, 1969: 97-8).

The remainder of the data were collected by means of interviews and detailed discussions with individual managers of the host-company. By far the largest group of managers interviewed were those who had declared five to six months earlier that amongst their personal employment strategies was an interest in becoming self-employed. This strategy allowed a longitudinal element to be introduced into the data collection and so reduced the reliance upon cross-sectional data. It is these data collected by questionnaire and by interview which form the basis of the analyses presented below.

ANALYSIS

Numbers wanting to become self-employed

One of the most surprising initial findings was the large number of managers who counted 'self-employment' amongst their personal employment strategies (Table 1). However, of the seventy managers who stated that they were considering becoming self-employed, only eighteen of them were pursuing only this option. These eighteen managers were all over forty-

145

TABLE 1

EMPLOYMENT STRATEGIES ADOPTED

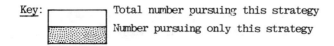

0   100

1. More or less exactly the
    same as present position

2. Not exactly same as
    present position but
    one in the same
    professional field.

3. A wide range of jobs of
    professional and
    executive status.

4. Almost any kind of job.

5. A specific kind of job,
    not the same as present
    position.

6. Some form of self-
    employment e.g.
    consultancy,
    manufacturing.

7. Not pursuing any form
    of employment

    (n = 229)

    Key: ┌──────────┐   Total number pursuing this strategy
         │▒▒▒▒▒▒▒▒▒▒│   Number pursuing only this strategy
         └──────────┘

146

five years of age and in a number of cases were already running a
business on a part time basis. The three most popular parallel employment strategies pursued with self-employment were: 'not exactly your
present position but one in the same professional field' (20); 'a
specific kind of job, not the same as your present position' (11); and,
'a wide range of jobs of professional and executive status' (10).
Pursuing two employment strategies, one of which is self-employment, is
not as contradictory as it may at first appear. The majority of individuals who were considering becoming consultants (31 cases) in their
own right were at the same time also seeking employment with a consultancy firm. The line dividing both types of employment - paid employment with a consultancy firm and being a consultant in one's own right -
is perceived as being very hazy. In fact, some managers could see no
difference between either of them.

Characteristics of those wanting to become self-employed

Some of the distinctive characteristics and related factors relating to
those managers considering self-employment can be summarised as follows:

a) The majority had worked for their present employer for
   over half of their working lives (87 per cent of cases)
   which usually means 15-20 years.

b) The majority of the managers had always worked for large
   firms (55 per cent).

c) A significant minority of managers' parents had been,
   and in some cases were still, self-employed (23 per cent)
   but the majority of their working parents had worked for
   similar large firms (55 per cent).

d) The majority of managers had made no attempt to become
   self-employed prior to being interviewed (58 per cent)
   though nearly 20 per cent had made some attempt and a
   further 20 per cent had actually run (or were running) an
   'own account' business of some description.

e) Most managers had only thought about becoming self-employed
   over the previous year to eighteen months (58 per cent)
   while some could date their thinking back ten years or
   more (10 per cent).

f) Relatively more managers interested in self-employment

147

(directly) supervised (more) staff than those exhibiting
no interest in self-employment (47 per cent of managers
interested in self-employment supervise six or more staff
compared with 31 per cent for the other managers).

g) While the sample of managers was drawn from all of the
possible departments, groups and works (62 in all which
are normally reduced to seven main groups) the ones with
the largest proportions of managers interested in self-
employment were the 'R & T' and 'safety and security'
departments and two works.

h) As a reflection of the seniority of the managers interested
in self-employment, a higher proportion of them had company
cars (32 per cent) than those not interested in self-
employment (18 per cent).

i) Over the past thirty years the host-company, and the multinational company of which it forms a part, had undergone a
number of major reorganisations which had resulted in the
relocation of employees, and it was more likely to find
those managers interested in self-employment amongst this
group.

j) Again, as a reflection of the higher seniority of the managers
interested in self-employment, a greater proportion of them
had complete autonomy over at least one or more business
policy areas (46 per cent) as compared to their counterparts
not interested in self-employment (36 per cent).

k) A number of specific business policy areas emerged which
tended to differentiate between the two groups of managers.
Of those managers interested in self-employment a larger
proportion had complete autonomy over capital expenditure
(36 per cent) than their counterparts not interested in self-
employment (14 per cent of cases), while a greater proportion
of this latter group could change suppliers (63 per cent)
than could the former group (40 per cent).

l) As a general rule of thumb, those managers who had been with
the host-company five or less years were almost wholly seeking some form of paid employment, while those with more
than thirty years service were interested in self-employment.
The large number of managers between these lower and upper

148

limits were equally distributed between both interest,
and non-interest in self-employment.

m) Those managers interested in self-employment were members
of marginally more professional bodies (which reflects
the greater representation of technologists amongst them)
than their counterparts who were not interested in self-
employment.

There are a large number of comparisons that can be made between the
two groups of managers; those interested, with those not interested in
self-employment. Many more such comparisons are required before the
descriptive analyses are complete, and at this stage it would appear
that many of the more important differences between the two groups of
managers are to be found in their lives outside the workplace setting.
One important element of these on-going analyses will be the factors
which have enhanced and impeded individual manager's employment search
strategies e.g. willingness to move, financial commitments, level of
savings, etc. How many managers, for example, can be classified as
'reluctant would-be entrepreneurs'? (Cross and Gibb, 1982)

Business Ideas of Those Wanting to Become Self-employed

Overall, there was a marked absence of ideas for a small business that
might result in the establishment of a business of any scale. The
majority of ideas were little more than ideas to become employed on an
'own account' basis, and very few would immediately result in the
establishment of a manufacturing firm. Moreover, very few of the
businesses could be related to the present employment of the managers.
Thus, the only 'spin-offs' from the company would appear at this stage
to be composed of managerial abilities and expertise exploited as
consultants.

It would appear (at first sight) that a relationship might exist
between the type of business idea and the age of the manager (see Table
2). The proportion of managers pursuing the employment strategy of
becoming a consultant (on an own account basis), for example, was
greater as the age of manager increased. There are a number of possible
interpretations which can be offered to account for this situation.

149

TABLE 2

BUSINESS IDEA AND AGE OF MANAGER

Age	Business Idea	Total
Up to 29	Consultant/retail business, consultant, beauty salon, don't know (all one case each)	4
30–34	Hotel	1
35–39	Consultant (2), small manufacturer (1)	3
40–44	Consultant, small holding, sailing, self-employment agency, boarding house, don't know (all one case each)	6
45–49	Consultant (4), hotel (2), garden centre (2), writing and retail businesses, brewery, leisure industry, antique shop, stamp dealer, don't know (all one case each)	14
50–54	Consultant (9), don't know (4), post-office (2), market gardening, retailing, gardener, painting, letting holiday cottages, antique and art dealer, property restoration, small business (all one case each)	23
55+	Consultant (13), market gardening, service to farmers, retail business, landscape gardener, craft workshop, furniture restorer, consultant/retail business, furniture design, arts and crafts, post-office, don't know (all one case each)	24

First, the longer the career history, the more defined are the abilities and capabilities of the individual. It would therefore seem reasonable to suggest that individuals in the latter part of their careers will know, to either a greater or lesser extent, 'what they can do' and 'what they want to do' (Porter and Lawler, 1968; Thomason,

1978, 195-234). The expectations of this group of managers will be
quite distinct from those who are just embarking on their careers and
still experiencing socialisation (Van Maanen and Schein, 1979; Schein,
1978, 81-111). These differences in expectations are in part a result
of the variations in the lengths of the respective careers, and also as
a result of the diminuition of the range of career options available as
a career develops - the Funnelling Effect (Hotchkiss, 1979). However,
managers who are in the middle and latter parts of their careers will
have acquired a specific skill (that is, if they are to acquire a rec-
ognisable skill at all) which is recognised both within 'the internal
labour market' (Doeringer and Piore, 1971) and by other employers, i.e.,
these managers have acquired an ability and have proven their capacity
to perform a recognised task (or series of tasks). Both an ability and
a capacity to perform a task can be regarded as an asset (or as a
personal investment) which can be exploited either by its explicit use
as a self-employed consultant (or similar), or by its implicit use with
another employer. Such a choice of employment form is generally not
open to managers whose careers are still developing.

A number of other interpretations are also possible. It could be
argued, and this is the second interpretation offered, that the willingness of managers to change career (possibly after a period of training)
decreases with age. Embarking on a new career late in working life
will not be regarded as a sound proposition for many managers. There
may be, therefore, a deterrent factor in operation which 'pushes' the
older manager to a similar job in a new setting (if available) or
'attracts' him to the idea of exploiting an existing hobby. The latter
two processes are further influenced by the decreasing financial commitments of many of the older managers e.g. their children have left home,
they probably own their home, etc. There are other possible interpretations, and the above two are offered as examples rather than, at
this stage, an attempt to encompass the profusion of explanations needed
to accommodate the behaviour of individual managers.

Methods Adopted by Those Wanting to Become Self-employed

By and large the managers who have evaluated the possibility of becoming
self-employed can be divided into two distinct groups: those who had
made a major effort and those who had made none. By far the larger of

the two groups comprises of those managers who had made little or no effort to become self-employed other than to speculate on what they might do and attend presentations arranged by the Resettlement Group (approximately 35-40 cases). The remaining managers can be further divided into those who were committed to becoming self-employed (18 cases), and those who had sought information from a number of sources and made a good deal of effort to establish the realities and potential of becoming self-employed (12-17 cases).

The main sources of information and advice used to date have been friends and colleagues, the local small business club, and the advisory bodies, e.g. COSIRA, DoI Counselling Service, etc. Many of the managers who had not sought any information at the time of writing were still developing their thoughts on self-employment. For some this was the first time they had ever considered becoming self-employed. The change of attitudes (and aspirations) needed to move from being a large company employee to becoming self-employed are quite great. Initial thoughts of self-employment need to be positively reinforced if progress is to be made from ideas of self-employment to action needed for self-employment. One of the barriers identified by managers in interviews was one of perception. Becoming self-employed did not match up to the image they had of themselves.

Reasons Expressed by Those Wanting to Become Self-employed

The reasons why individual managers wanted to become self-employed varied widely and are difficult to unravel from one another. For some, becoming self-employed is the fulfilment of a cherished ambition, while for others it was seen as an enjoyable and respectable means of easing themselves into retirement (Shaw and Grubbs, 1981; Weinrauch, 1980). For another group, self-employment was seen as an option of last resort. Having tried a number of applications for jobs elsewhere and failed, these managers were (having been forced to) tentatively considering self-employment.

The development and definition of the business idea very much reflects the reasons given for becoming, or considering becoming, self-employed. For example, those managers who were tentatively considering the merits (or lack of them) of self-employment suffered from what bankers call the

'post-office syndrome'. Their ideas were ill-defined and often
ignored many of the pitfalls of self-employment. The notion of becoming self-employed had become more important than the mechanics and
operations of the business which would support that state of employment.
Their business ideas were drawn from the most readily available
examples of self-employment, e.g. the post-office, the window cleaner,
local shop keeper, etc. However, what had occurred with this group of
managers was that they at least acknowledged the possibility of
becoming self-employed, which might not have otherwise been the case.

Barriers Identified by Those Wanting to Become Self-employed

As was noted earlier, one of the main barriers for many of the managers
was perceptual. The self image many managers developed is one applicable to the large company and not the small company. There was also an
intellectual difference between the two work settings. In the large
company, some managers argued you could tackle 'real', 'significant'
and 'meaningful' problems which required time and money, neither of
which would be available in the small company (Welsh and White, 1981).
These arguments were especially prevalent amongst those managers who
were reluctantly considering self-employment. Other common problems
were loss of status, loss of income and loss of pension rights.

However, those managers who were committed to becoming self-employed,
whilst mentioning the above barriers, had identified more specific
problems with their business itself. The lack of specific skills or
knowledge was a common one. Again, even these barriers were a little
remote from the hardware of the business itself. For example, few
managers had put specific proposals to their bank manager, and premises
had rarely been sought by the managers whose businesses could not
operate from home.

At this stage of the research it can be suggested that there are
would-be independent entrepreneurs to be found in large companies.
There is stress on the word found, because some of the managers dealt
with have been very positively encouraged into thinking about becoming
self-employed. Once a manager who expressed some interest in becoming
self-employed had been found, he was being encouraged to think 'self-
employment'. Whether this process has an impact will not be known for

some time, but the first signs are that it might, and more new businesses be established then might have occurred otherwise.

SUMMARY AND POLICY IMPLICATIONS

The preliminary findings from the current programme of work indicate that a significant minority of large company employees, managers in this case, under certain conditions, are willing to seriously consider becoming self-employed (Robson, 1981). The number of new businesses to emerge as a result of this process is, however, neither likely to be great, nor are they in turn likely to employ large numbers of people. Of the seventy managers considered here, it seems that as many as thirty five businesses might finally emerge. This total would have been probably less than ten had not the company embarked upon what must be regarded as an enlightened resettlement policy offering positive aid and assistance.

But What Does This All Mean For Policy?

Probably the simplest lesson to be learnt from the work is that a far greater number of people, managers in this case, could become self-employed. Self-employment is not a specialist category of employment reserved for the few, it is a realistic employment option open to a far greater number of individuals than has hitherto been expected. If such an employment option is realistically and actively presented to those individuals considering a career change (or having such a decision forced upon them) more people might consider, and embark upon, a career of self-employment. And it can be argued that, under certain conditions, the effort required to promote self-employment will be rewarded.

This effort may, however, need to be matched with the provision of wider access to ideas for businesses if small companies of any immediate size (in employment terms) are to be launched. This in particular may be of interest to those at the younger end of the age spectrum. The present research, for example, tentatively demonstrates that the more 'substantial ideas' are found in the middle age band, although the age distribution as a whole is skewed towards the older age bands where pre-retirement and hobby type businesses are more likely to emerge. The

154

research also indicates that large company resettlement schemes can exercise an influence on the thinking of individual managers, and upon this influence could therefore be built opportunities to consider more substantial (in employment terms) business ideas. The project work needed to seek out and develop such ideas could be built into resettlement options. Wider horizons might also be given to such managers by building into resettlement programmes the possibility of working for a period in a small firm. This might provide the 'transition' between leaving a large company and setting up on one's own. Moreover, a more positive attempt to develop interest in self-employment and to unearth would-be entrepreneurs could be to devise various internal stimuli e.g. SYOB competitions.

In conclusion, probably the most significant of all of the findings is that resettlement programmes can bring forward substantial numbers of employees with interests in pursuing careers outside of the company and who are also therefore 'open to change'. If, in the interests of efficiency and competitiveness, labour forces of large companies must be reduced then positive efforts to achieve the desired results without unemployment are at least worth considering. And, if into this type of resettlement programme can be added support for motivation, the development of abilities and of viable ideas for small business creation, there could be a positive bonus indeed. It is therefore possible to adopt relatively modest schemes in company dominated labour markets to lessen some of the worst effects of a major plant closure or contraction.

ACKNOWLEDGEMENT

The author would like to acknowledge the financial support provided by the Social Science Research Council for the research reported in this paper and also the extensive assistance and advice given by the host-company, co-investigator Dr. Allan Gibb, and Vivienne Williams.

REFERENCES

Andrisani, P.J., Longitudinal research and labour force behaviour. Introduction and Overview , *Journal of Economics and Statistics,* Vol. 32, No.2, 1980.

Chinitz, B., Contrasts in Agglomeration: New York and Pittsburgh , *American Economic Review,* Vol.51, 1961.

Cross, M. and Gibb, A.A., Research into the Entrepreneurial Base of Large Firms in the Northern Region , SSRC Final Report Grant No. 6241/2 1982.

Doeringer, P.B. and Piore, M.J., *Internal Labour Markets and Manpower Analysis*, Heath, Lexington, 1971.

Hotchkiss, L., A Conceptual-Measurement Model for Career Expectations , paper presented to the Annual Meeting of the Mid West Sociological Society, Minneapolis, 1979.

Porter, L.W. and Lawler, E.E., *Managerial Attitudes and Performance*, Homewood, Ill. Irwin-Dorsey, 1968.

Robson, E., Face to Face with Change in the British Steel Industry. A Recipe with Potential . Paper presented to International Committee on Occupational Mental Health Symposium, Heidelberg, 1981.

Schein, E.H., *Process Consultation: Its Role in Organisation Development*, A Mass., Addison-Wesley, 1969.

Schein, E.H., *Career Dynamics: Matching Individual and Organizational Needs*, Mass., Addison-Wesley, 1978.

Shaw, J.B. and Grubbs, L.L., The Process of Retiring: Organizational Entry in Reverse , *Academy of Management Review*, Vol.6, No.1, 1981.

Thomason, G., Individual Goals and Expectations in Work , Chapter 4, in Thomason, G., *A Textbook of Personnel Management*, London, IPM, 1978, 3rd Edition.

Van Maanen, J. and Schein, E.H., Toward a Theory of Organizational Socialization , in Staw, B.M. and Cummings, L.L. eds. *Research in Organizational Behaviour*, Greenwich, Conn., JAI Press, Vol.1, 1979.

Weinrauch, J.D., The Second Time Around: Entrepreneurship as a Mid-Career Alternative , *Journal of Small Business Management*, Vol.18, No.1, 1980.

Welsh, J.A. and White, J.F., A Small Business is Not a Little Big Business , *Harvard Business Review*, Vol.59, No.4, 1981.

IV INDUSTRIAL RELATIONS

,and the general economic performance of that industry and the
at large. In the specific case of the industry from which we
r evidence, the clothing industry, which has a large proportion
n workers, it is necessary to draw both on theories of the dual
market, and on the situation of dependency in which many firms
industry find themselves, if we are to understand the setting for
nt labour quiesence.

SM AND DEPENDENCY

evelopment of dual labour market analysis derived from work carried
n the USA in the 1950s concerning the persistence of low paid
rs of the labour force (particularly black workers), in an other-
affluent and booming society. The work of Kerr (1975) has been
icularly influential.

thin Kerr's analysis can be found the central pillars around which
labour market theory has been constructed. These can be itemised
follows:

a) The labour market is an entity subdivided into various
   non-competing groups.

b) The driving force behind this subdivision is the increased
   size and bureaucracy of industrial units.

c) The conscious actions of both managements, and workers (in
   the form of trade unions), are important in determining
   the structure and functioning of internal labour markets
   and other forms of 'social enclosure'.

With few changes, dual labour market theorists have accepted Kerr's
analysis and concentrated on explaining why sub-divisions should have
come about, rather than questioning the categories that Kerr defines.
It is, however, necessary to note that there is not a single, homo-
geneous school of dual labour market theory. For the sake of simplicity
we intend to examine only those strands associated with Doeringer and
Piore (1981) and Reich, Gordon and Edwards (1980).

The 'orthodox school' (Doeringer and Piore, 1981) are mainly concerned
with accounting for the low earnings of particular groups of workers
(women and, more especially, blacks) in the US labour market. They conclude that such groups of 'disadvantaged' workers tended to find jobs

Beyond Bolton — Industrial Relations in the Small Firm
MICHAEL SCOTT AND ALISTAIR RAINNIE

A widely held view of industrial relations in the small firm is one of
harmony based on ease of communications, flexibility of work roles and
the identification of the worker with company objectives. This
picture was adopted uncritically by the Bolton Report and its findings
have been generally accepted ever since:

> In many respects the small firm provides a better environment
> for the employee than is possible in most large firms. Although
> physical working conditions may sometimes be inferior in small
> firms, most people prefer to work in a small group where
> communications present fewer problems - the employee in a small
> firm can more easily see the relation between what he is doing
> and the objectives and performance of the firm as a whole.
> Where individual management is more direct and flexible, work-
> ing rules can be varied to suite the individual. (Bolton
> Report 1971: 21)

The necessity of investigating this conventional view of industrial
relations in small firms is reinforced by the important role that all
major political parties assign to small businesses in the struggle to
drag the British economy out of the present recession.

Beyond Bolton

The conventional wisdom of 'harmony' lies within an ideology of consen-
sus and paternalism which has a long tradition, going back to the
nineteenth century romanticised entrepreneur. (There is an extensive
literature on what may be called 'let us now praise famous businessmen'
from Samuel Smiles onwards. See Lewis and Stewart, 1958: Chapter 2.)
Its antecedents would also include the work of Schumacher. More immediately, Bolton appears to have drawn heavily on the work of Ingham.

Although one can find instances of disquiet with this conventional
wisdom throughout the ten years since the publication of the Bolton

Report (see, for example, Henderson and Johnson, 1974; Nash, 1980), it is only in the last three years that serious attempt has been made in the literature, notably by Curran and Stanworth (1979a), to question the alleged 'harmony' in small firms.

Curran and Stanworth have adequately reviewed the literature and it is therefore only necessary to provide the briefest summary of the arguments in the debate. Ingham concluded:

> That the large plant workers were economistic and instru-
> mental in their orientation to work; that is, they were
> very sensitive to the economic (especially wages) aspects
> of their employment and less concerned with non economic
> factors. On the other hand the small firm men appeared
> to be setting their acceptable wage level at a much lower
> level and, at the same time, demanded a higher level of
> non economic rewards (non economistic-expressive orienta-
> tion). Therefore, in both large and small organisations
> there was a high level of congruence between the workers'
> wants and expectations (orientations) and the organisa-
> tional reward structure. (Ingham, 1970: 143)

Furthermore,

> The more informal organisations at work and more extensive
> management worker interaction in the small firms provided
> the structural conditions for a relatively high level of
> moral involvement. Many workers in the small firms were
> seen to define their work roles not merely in terms of cash
> nexus; but also as obligations and duties. (Ingham, 1970:
> 143)

This constitutes the part of Ingham's analysis that the Bolton Report (1971) adopted uncritically. We should remind ourselves, however, that Ingham's sample of small firm workers was restricted to a narrow range of technology (unit and small batch production in light engineering) and included only skilled and semi-skilled male workers aged over 21. In many respects, therefore, this is substantially unrepresentative of all small firms.

Curran and Stanworth's work, by contrast, is based on interviews with 145 shop floor workers ranging in age from sixteen to over sixty and representing all skill levels. (However, this did not include any women.) The workers were employed in two industries, printing and electronics. The first of these is old established, highly unionised, and has a history of severe conflict between managers and workers. The latter is new, has a low level of unionisation and low levels of worker-management conflict. These two sharply contrasting industries were

chosen deliberately to assess the importance o[f]
influences on worker-management relationships a[nd]
entirely related to size of firm. Curran and S[tanworth]
from 88 interviews with a controlled sample of e[mployees in]
two large firms, one in each of the industries.

Their main findings include:

a) No support for Ingham's view that workers [in small firms]
   are self selected in terms of non economist[ic]
   orientation. Rather that occupational place[ment with]
   an emphasis on social relationships with sig[nificant others]
   (Curran and Stanworth, 1979b)

b) Evidence that for these two industries at lea[st, the influence]
   of industrial sub-cultures reverses the expect[ed relationship]
   between the size of firm and the workers' emph[asis on]
   intrinsic aspects of work.(Curran and Stanwort[h,]

c) Evidence that horizontal social relationships b[etween workers]
   within small firms are only marginally closer th[an in large]
   firms, coupled with evidence that, for these ind[ustries at]
   least, the small firm workers have low levels of [non-]
   work contacts with workmates. (Curran and Stanwor[th,]

d) Evidence that vertical social relationships are in[fluenced]
   more by industrial sub-culture values than by size[, and]
   that the alleged special identification of small fi[rm]
   workers with management goals is not supported. [(Curran]
   and Stanworth, 1979a)

d) Evidence that the 'idea of a sharp difference betwee[n the]
   attitudes of workers in small and large firms to trad[e]
   unions and to collective bargaining has been grossly [over-]
   drawn'. (Curran and Stanworth, 1981b)

The critique developed by Curran and Stanworth of the approa[ch to]
industrial relations in small firms adopted by Bolton and Ingh[am]
implied that a 'more structural approach' was necessary, incor[porating]
'a whole set of wider influences which impinge on both the smal[l firm]
worker and his employer and their relations with each other'. [(Curran]
and Stanworth, 1980)

It will be argued in this paper that the industrial relations p[osition]
in a small firm cannot be divorced from the position of that firm

that were systematically different from those of the more 'advantaged' workers.

By definition, 'disadvantaged' (secondary sector) workers are employed in enterprises where wages are low, working conditions are poor, employment is often unstable and opportunities for on-the-job training and advancement are severely limited; by contrast 'advantaged' (primary sector) workers tend to receive higher pay, relatively secure employment and on-the-job training that leads to higher earnings.

Labour market duality therefore 'results largely from difference in recruitment, promotion and training practices'. In the secondary sector firms have open internal labour markets providing little or no opportunity for training or promotion. The primary sector workers are occupants of andparticipants in a relatively closed or structured internal labour market which has limited entry to specific jobs and then relies on training and promotion to fill remaining posts.

'Internal' labour markets have developed, therefore, as skills become more and more specific to a particular firm and the costs involved in on-the-job training rise to such a level that any significant amount of labour turnover represents an unacceptable price in terms of replacement training costs etc. Therefore a firm will attempt to encourage the development of a stable labour force, by paying wage rates above the 'market level'. The restrictions on entry imposed by the internal market structure and the diminished influence of the market level on the firm's wage payment structure will tend to create a section of the labour market that is relatively independent of the labour market as a whole.

It should be noted, however, that only a few firms (oligopolies and monopolies) are in a position to grant to sections of their labour force the 'privileges' inherent in the primary sector of the dual labour market.

The importance of the secondary sector in this process is that it allows the primary sector to ride out periods of instability in the economy by farming out some proportion of uncertainty onto firms in the secondary sector. The relative stability of the oligopolistic sector, the stability which allows it to develop internal labour markets, is achieved partly by their market position and partly by either subcon-

tracting to the secondary sector or by employing workers from the
secondary sector on a temporary basis.

In the 'orthodox' approach outlined above, the labour force is essentially passive; workers appear either as a commodity with particular
skills desired by oligopolistic firms, or else as little more than
factory fodder in the unstable secondary sector.

Reich, Gordon and Edwards (1980) attempted to extend the concept of
managerial control of the labour force (in the orthodox approach con-
stituting little more than an attempt to create stability in one particular sector) into a far more political concept. They define labour
market segmentation as:

> .....the historical process whereby political-economic
> forces encourage the division of the labour market into
> separate sub markets or segments distinguished by different
> labour market characteristics and behaviour rules.(Reich
> et al, 1980: 383)

Segmentation, they argue, arose during the transition from competitive
to monopoly capitalism (the period roughly from the 1880s to the First
World War). It did so because this transition, through the process of
de-skilling, threatened to bring about a homogenisation of the labour
force whose increasingly proletarian character threatened a widespread
and growing opposition to capitalism. To cover this threat employers
actively pursued a 'divide and rule' tactic, based on labour market
regulation.

It was not simply the segmentation of the labour force that divided
the working class - the operation of internal labour markets strengthened this process by instilling into sections of the labour force a 'hier-
archy fetishism'. This fetishism was designed to create a craving for
better jobs and more status, thus driving a wedge between workers and
limiting the possibility of the creation of class consciousness.   In
this way, workers are divided not only between primary and secondary
sectors but also within each sector. This division has a dual role,
firstly the mere existence of the secondary sector raises the status of
those in the primary sector and secondly, as those sections of the
labour force most discriminated against (e.g. blacks and women) are concentrated in the secondary sector, low wages can continue to be paid to
these sections of the labour force without running the risk of generalised class opposition.

There is however, a danger inherent in the radical approach, that of developing a 'conspiracy theory' to account for the segmentation of the labour market. As Rubery has argued:

> This approach directs attention away from the particular circumstances which induced individual employers to develop internal labour markets where workers earn above the external market wage. Avoidance of imminent industrial action, installation of new technology or an attempt to gain some competitive advantage over rival firms, are much more likely to underlie these differentials rather than some strategy to avoid long term, widespread class opposition. (1980: 250)

It can be seen therefore, that there are important differences in the way various academics have analysed the response of workforce and management to uncertainty. The point to bear in mind is that, although these schools have differing views as to why labour market duality came into being, all of them accept, with minor modifications, Kerr's categorisation of the segments of the labour market, and all concentrate their focus of attention on what are variously described as advantaged, central or primary sector workers. It therefore follows that, if doubt is placed on the rigid division of the labour market, then dual labour market theory will begin to lose its coherence.

Blackburn and Mann's study (1979) of the labour market in Peterborough in fact did come to a number of conclusions that run against the hypotheses of dual labour market theory. They acknowledge that internal labour markets do exist but argue that they do not form 'stable quasi hereditory strata': rather Blackburn and Mann prefer to call them 'non-stable groupings', and crucially, whilst concluding that:

> The oldest industrial nation, ethnically homogeneous, with severe restrictions on immigration, Britain is obviously not a major candidate for a divided manual working class. (1979: 301)

they go on to argue that:

> Our analysis shows that only sex is a major stable division. (Blackburn and Mann: 301)

Whilst accepting that internal labour markets and so on do actually exist and do have an important role to play in dividing the working class, when put into historical perspective (See Hobsbawn, 1964. The notion of 'labour aristocracy' conforms well with the ideas of 'primary' sector workers.) Blackburn and Mann's characterisation of internal labour markets as 'non stable groupings' would seem more applicable than the rigid categorisation adopted by dual labour market theorists.

We must now look, if only briefly, at the effect on management and labour force in small businesses of the dependent relationship between large and small firms. As we have already indicated, the relationship between large and small firms is important:

> ....large firms are able to bypass or forestall internal technical reorganisations when adjusting to changed product demand by increasing or decreasing their co-operative relations with small firms. Similarly they are able to bypass the disruptive consequences of central worker lay-offs by reducing co-operative relations in times of adversity. (Friedman, 1977: 105)

This has important consequences for workers in small firms in two different ways. Firstly, because of the flexibility of co-operative relations (the degree of dependency) of the small firm with the large, the small firm owner-manager cannot afford to grant to his labour force the degree of latitude possible in the large firm. In other words, management style will be limited to the control of the adaptability of labour through close supervision and the allowing of minimal respons-ibility. Secondly, the non-central workers in this sector are even more vulnerable than their equivalents in the large firms, in that they are employed in unstable firms. Their position is made more difficult by the fact that the lack of restrictions to entry to their jobs and their relative lack of skill make them more open to pressures from the pool of unemployed or potentially employable, thus forcing them to accept the more authoritarian managerial style and lower wages.

The importance of this analysis is that it lays a theoretical basis on which one can argue with the Bolton Report's findings. For example, Bolton took as one element in its three part definition of a small firm, the independence of that unit. We would argue that this concept has to be defined more closely.

The degree of dependency can and does have important effects on man-agement strategy, workforce stability and thus the possibilities of developing workforce collective organisation, as we shall see when we examine the state of labour relations in small clothing factories.

Much empirical work has been carried out in recent years into the
industrial relations practices of large firms, mainly in engineering and
related industries, and employing male workers. We have deliberately
chosen to look at current labour relations in an industry which has a
predominance of small scale units and which has a mainly female workforce.

There is relatively little structural concentration of employment in
the clothing industry in Britain (Department of Employment Gazette,
1978). In 1976, 62 per cent of the establishments in the industry em-
employed 25 or less employees. The concentration of employees in establishments employing less than 200 workers is far greater (69%) in the
clothing industry than it is for all the production industries (44%).

Within the North East, there were, in April 1977, 22,746 employees in
185 establishments, the average size of each establishment being 123
employees. Our own figures suggest a continued decline to just over
18,000 employees in 130 establishments in early 1981.

A third of employment in the industry in the North East is in small
firms. More importantly 90 per cent of employees in the industry are
women. Furthermore, 15 per cent of these women are under nineteen and
13 per cent are in part time employment. We have therefore, a sample of
small firms in an industry largely employing women, many of whom are
young and/or are employed on a part time basis. In making generic
comments on industrial relations in small firms, it will be from this
sample that we shall be drawing our examples.

IMAGE AND REALITY

Owners and Managers

The owners and managers we talked to echoed the conventional wisdom set
out in Bolton, usually emphasising that the interpersonal aspects of
small groups were their greatest advantage:

> Most industrial relations relate to your ability to
> communicate; it's difficult to talk to a large number
> of people. In a small place you can talk to individuals
> unless they are real hotheads. (sic). Once you get over

two hundred people there is no personal contact, people
are more like machines.

There does not seem to be any difference in this attitude between
those persons who were the owners of the firms, and those who were managing small units on behalf of absent owners. We realise that 'ownership' and 'management' are significantly different functions, especially
in the context of capital versus labour, but both groups, irrespective
of their previous career lines shared the conventional wisdom.

The stress on teamwork, however, began to break down when detailed
questions were asked about wage payment systems, labour turnover,
grievance procedures and trade union organisation. What began to emerge
instead, was a picture of highly authoritarian management style. For
instance, one of the points always emphasised in any discussion of the
advantages of small scale is the 'personal touch':

> They come round to my house, I know them all personally,
> I know their problems.

However, it rapidly became clear that it was alright to have problems,
as long as they did not affect the amount of work done. Yet with an
almost totally female labour force, for many of the workforce family
commitments could cause problems:

> We understand that some will have family problems, but they
> have got to realise the pitfalls involved in coming out to
> work - who is going to look after the kids and so on. We
> have to instill discipline in them.

It soon became clear that the advantages of scale and having a pre-
dominately female labour force were perceived in terms of gains to management rather than some overall 'team' concept:

> Knowing names gives you an advantage in dealing with problems.
> They think, 'Oh. he knows me' and you are half way there.
> That's the advantage of a female labour force, you can get
> round them, you can flannel them, get to know them better.
> Men would be suspicious straight away. It's easier if you
> want them to do a bit of overtime for example. I think
> they are smashing.

The main problem that the managers associated with their workforce was
not a function of size as they saw it, but rather a function of the
gender of their workforce. High labour turnover (up to 42 per cent per
annum in our sample), the main problem identified by managers, was due,
they said, solely to family problems and pregnancy. (Labour turnover
in the industry as a whole reached a level of 50 per cent in 1969,

though declining through the 1970s). The managers belief that the reasons for labour turnover are family related is flatly contradicted however by research carried out for the Clothing Economic Development Committee in the early 1970s. Questioning operatives in the clothing industry as to the reasons why so many people left, 30 per cent of the women gave the main reason as boredom, a further 25 per cent mentioned looking for more money and 25 per cent suggested 'that other aspects of work were involved' (Elliston Research Associates: 5).

It became increasingly clear that a large proportion of labour turn-over was caused by a hunt for higher wages, no matter how marginal. Some managers recognise this situation. Talking about why he had taken on part timers, one manager explained that it was because another cloth-ing factory had opened up nearby (between one and two miles away) that had paid slightly higher wages and provided transport to and from work. He had had to raise his own wage levels and provide transport to counter act the effect of his own workers leaving to join the rival.

Evidence such as this certainly fits better with analyses of the labour process in the secondary sector of the labour market, rather than with Ingham's 'non-economistic expressive' orientations model. However, the picture of high labour turnover has altered dramatically over the past two years. High unemployment and near collapse of the clothing industry has meant women hanging onto whatever jobs they can get.

This situation has been exacerbated by the position that many small clothing factories find themselves in, in relation to the large retail companies. One Trade magazine has commented that:

> The partnership between Marks and Spencers and its UK
> clothing suppliers is misunderstood by those outside
> the industry who like to stick a 'love-hate' label on
> the relationship.
> .... The relationship stemming back to the
> 1920s is one of mutual interdependence whereby each
> needs each other. Yet, in return for sizeable orders
> placed, suppliers have to accept disciplines that would
> be quite beyond the pale by other clothing manufacturers.
> (Clothing Manufacturer, 1981: 17)

Owners do not willingly surrender control of their firms, but by surrendering an element of control over their own production, the small firm can become at least partially protected from the rigours of the open market. The protection is provided by large, long term and

169

recurrent orders that shield the small firm from having to scratch
around for unpredictable and unprofitable short runs.

The relationship between the small firms and the large retail outlets
does have certain advantages as far as the women who work in the small
clothing factories are concerned, in that bonus[1] (an important part of
take home pay) is more certain and easier to calculate on long runs.

Yet the existence of a bonus system means that workers rely heavily
on other people working at a rate sufficient to allow them to keep up
their own bonus rate. However, this does not aid the establishment of
a collective consciousness:

> .... you work for yourself you see .... if anybody was
> off you had to work twice as hard if you wanted the same
> bonus .... There's a lot of greed in the incentives isn't
> there? You know, the girls working for themselves, it's
> grab, grab, grab you know.

Union and Steward

It has been argued that 'the world view of the owner manager has been
repeatedly found to stress independence, antipathy towards large external organisations and a dislike of theory as opposed to practice'
(Curran and Stanworth, 1979: 427). From our experience of managers in
the clothing industry 'antipathy towards large external organisations'
is a very mild description of their attitude to trade unions ('They're
all extremists').

The general antipathy to trade unions at large was significantly not
reflected in attitudes to the specific union which represents most
workers in the industry. The attitude to the NUTGW is one of indiffer-
ence or at worst, mild irritation.

So why is the NUTGW acceptable to managers where trade unions generally are viewed as a total anathema? The union full time officers have
a number of explanations. Firstly, the make up and tradition of the
industry:

> but then again we get lads (as full time officers)....
> who've maybe been convenors in light engineering....
> they are literally appalled by it (the organisation of
> the union and the role of the officer).... however, if
> they've got any gumption, most of them have, they can
> adapt .... they've got to do it more or less our way
> rather than the way they want to do it .....

Full time officials also despair of the calibre of their members, and management's attitude to shop stewards:

> I've got some places, take A for example.... and we've
> lost our shop stewards. So you put out the feelers. I
> go down and get two people - 'Oh. you've got to understand
> Mr. X we're not really shop stewards, we don't mind sort
> of liaising with people, we don't want to go to meetings,
> so if we've got problems we'll just ring you'. Well,
> what do you say?

How has the situation arisen whereby full time officials see their role as surrogate shop stewards, and why do the members and stewards appear to lack confidence in themselves?

To answer these questions we have to turn to the experience of shop stewards in these small clothing factories, and to examine how the difficulties faced by women trying to be active in trade union organisation manifest themselves in practice.

Firstly, a woman's involvement in active trade unionism can cause tensions within the family. This factor becomes particularly important when examining the question of attendance at branch meetings of the union. This is usually taken as an important part of any measure of union participation. The NUTGW organises its branches on a geographical basis. It is not unusual therefore to find that some stewards have to cover distances of ten miles or more to get to branch meetings. Meetings are usually held once a month at 7.00 p.m. This can create problems:

> It's too much to attend branch meetings. I've got a husband
> to look after.

Secondly, because of management prerogative over the key issue of bonus, the steward's power to 'deliver the goods' to her members where it matters is severely restricted:

> .... you see, the supervisor makes up the set-ups and she'll
> work through the old set-up - 'Oh. well, this is a new style,
> but I'll look through the old set-ups. Well, we've done a
> little bit of this and a little bit of that, so if we take
> that off there, a minute off there, that's your new timing'.
> But you always find her timings are very tight. And then
> now the girls are learning - "well, we're not happy and we
> want to be retimed". He comes and retimes us. True he
> looks at the clock on the wall, he works it out, looks at
> your sheet to find out how long it took you and he'll say -
> 'Well I rate you at this performance' but he cannot explain
> it to us how he's got it though, 'cos I know for a fact so
> much can be worked out methodically, but the next bit's guesswork...

For most workers, because of the perceived distance of the 'union' from the shop floor, the shop steward does not only represent the union, the steward is the union. Yet the stewards themselves see the union as remote, only to be brought in at times of extreme stress and to explain the annual wage settlement.

Given this sparse contact with the union at large and the very limited amount of control that stewards have within their own workplace, it is hardly surprising that workers within small factories are themselves apathetic about the union. Indeed, this is one of the stewards' major complaints:

> You go to management, you get them earlies, you get them
> tea breaks on an afternoon, which they are entitled to
> you know. Well, you're great in that respect. But there
> might be a time when they want an early, and because they're
> refused, 'Oh. the union does nothing for us, we're not
> bothered about the union'.

The complaint that 'you just can't win' is common to all stewards. However, if the power of the union as represented by the steward is seen to be incapable of influencing positively the contents of the weekly wage packet, if all that the power of the steward can do is to get a tea break you were entitled to in the first place, then it is hardly surprising that the union as embodied in the steward is seen to be largely irrelevant to the workers. Apathy, like commitment, does not fall from the skies; in this case it is rooted in the isolation of the steward from the union, the weakness of that union and the limited power of workplace trade unionism.

As Anna Pollett has said:

> They (the women) did not need to be bossed because they
> had their hands tied anyway. Tied by the incorporation
> of trade unionism into capital through a complex web of
> centralised procedures which were as distant as the stars
> and filtered down their effects through an invisible unknown
> bureaucracy. Power and decisions were somewhere 'out there',
> never in the factory, let alone the shop floor.
> (Pollett, 1979).

Even if a stewards' organisation does exist then management can find other ways to make a steward's life as difficult as possible and therefore still further limit their effectiveness:

> with all the new starters in, I'm trying to get round them
> all saying, 'Well do you want to join the union?' I must
> ask them 'Do you want to join the union?' .... I used the
> wrong words once and I had to go upstairs and get put on

172

the carpet for pressuring them .... Well, if I say to you
'Do you fancy joining the union?' - that was how I was
doing it - but they said I was pressuring them.

The restrictions placed on steward activity extend to the facilities
that they are able to extract from management to aid them in their job.
Access to telephone, duplicators, typewriters, filing cabinets and so
on is usually severely limited if not totally non-existent. Given their
lack of power and their isolation from the union, what is the steward's
view of her own role? The answer is 'very limited':

Nothing really, just being a voice for the girls more than
anything else.

One could not ask for a better contrast between the role of the Trade
Unions in large and small organisations. Hyman (1979) has suggested
the possibility, in large scale industry, of the assimilation of full
time convenors and shop stewards into official union structures and
away from their membership. In the clothing industry as a whole the
opposite problem is apparent. Stewards' activities are minimal in terms
of time spent and facilities at their disposal. The possibility of
developing to the stage of demanding full time status for shop stewards
is remote even in the larger, better organised factories. In the small
clothing factories the danger is not that the union members, having
wrested some control of their own jobs from management through their
own activity, are now faced with having their representatives withdrawn
from their control; rather that, having little or no control in the
first place, they face enormous obstacles to the development of their
own self activity. Not least of these problems is that whatever power
their union does possess is in the hands of people who are perceived to
be light years away from the shop floor. In other words, it is not a
question of how to defend what little control has been won, but how to
gain that bit of control they can see shop floor workers in other industries exercising. The stewards indeed recognise the weaknesses of
the union at a national level and their own position in the 'pecking
order'.

The instability of employment and their perceived powerlessness leaves
the stewards with a feeling of helplessness when faced with an autocratic management. This feeling of helplessness extends beyond the
confines of the individual workplace to the industry at large, resulting
in a feeling that even if they could organise militant mass action, it

would just be suicidal:

> If we had a walk out through shirts, people would just
> make a shirt last a little longer. And I feel striking
> in shirts you know, I think there's nothing at all to
> gain by it, you know. Because as I say you can't live
> without coal you know, it involves so much. Whereas
> shirts, I mean, if you can't get a shirt you buy a jumper,
> you know.

The picture we have painted of stewards faced by enormous obstacles
in the way of their attempts to build workplace union organisation flies
in the face of the conventional wisdom. However, there is a danger that
our analysis could be taken as implying that the task facing shop
stewards in small clothing factories is impossible. Obviously the
recent disputes at Lee Jeans and Glencoe Knitwear belie any such implication. In fact our analysis is not as deterministic as it would, at
first sight, seem to be. All that we are saying is that conflict does
exist in small clothing factories, but that because of the difficulties
in organising that we have outlined, it has tended to express itself in
terms of high labour turnover rather than trade union activity. Trade
union organisation is not impossible, but it is very difficult.

THE IMPORTANCE OF INTERNATIONAL TRADE

On a more general level we would argue that it is difficult to talk about
'the small firm' in any generic sense, particularly when examining
industrial relations. Market conditions, industrial sector, labour
force and dependency relationships will all play a vital part in shaping
industrial relations patterns. Furthermore these factors can change,
and therefore our ideas must be flexible enough to account for changing
circumstances. Managerial strategy, as far as it affects primary and
secondary sector workers, will be conditioned by the position of a
particular firm within an industry and that industry within the national
and international economy. Increasing competition, the development of
new technology, and generalised economic downturn can, and must, force
management to review the options open to them. In the case of small
clothing firms the over-riding factor affecting both managerial strategy
and worker responses has been increasing unemployment arising from
foreign competition. The dependency relationships between large and
small firms have also been significantly affected by this aspect of international trade.

TABLE 1

EMPLOYMENT IN THE UK CLOTHING INDUSTRY 1972-77 ('000's)

Year	1972	1973	1974	1975	1976	1977
Employment	340	327	322	307	303	295

Source: *International Labour Office, 1980: 9*

The clothing industry throughout Europe has been protesting for many years at the threat to its existence it believes is posed by the rise of clothing producers in the Third World (for the Trade Union response, see TUC, 1980 and TGWU 1980). The first signs of this development were beginning to be felt throughout Europe, but particularly in the UK from the 1960s onwards. The effect on employment is shown in Table 1.

However, it is the relationship between the decline in employment in the developed countries and the rise in exports from LDCs (lesser developed countries) that is of interest to us here. The situation is not quite as simple as at first sight it may appear to be. It is not simply a case of independent producers in the LDCs challenging independent producers in the developed countries. Frobel et al (1980) argue that in the case of West Germany, over 70 per cent of their sample of garment manufacturing companies maintained some sort of production abroad, particularly in the Third World, and that this trend has been accelerating since the middle 1960s. The firms have, in general, made use of 'free production zones' to aid their expansion. The authors conclude that the employment effects are limited as far as the interests of LDCs are concerned, the structure is biased towards unskilled labour, there is little or no transfer of technology and research and development is also limited. The only beneficiaries are the companies involved, taking advantage of generous state allowances and abundant cheap labour - mainly in the form of young unskilled women. As far as our analysis is concerned this would seem to suggest that, in the long term, the secondary sector in the clothing industry is going to shift from being concentrated in small factories in the developed world to the Third World.

Intra-national dependency relationships are being replaced by international dependencies with devastating effects on the employment poss-

ibilities of the secondary sector in developed countries. An ideology
of paternalism and years of strike free 'harmony' are not going to help
the worker in Jarrow when her fellow worker in Hong Kong is cheaper and
simply less trouble.

CONCLUSIONS

In this paper we have argued that certainly in the case of industrial
relations in small clothing firms, the 'small is beautiful' hypothesis
does not stand up to any sort of rigorous analysis. Yet the Ingham/
Bolton view of industrial relations in the small firm has over time
crystallised into a sort of unchallenged conventional wisdom.

This is hardly surprising given that the largely uncritical acceptance
of the advantages to the economy of a viable and healthy small firm
sector has translated itself, at least in terms of research, into a
concentration on stimulating entrepreneurship, business survival rates,
sources of finance, etc.   In other words, as long as we can ensure the
survival of an endangered species, the small businessman, we know that
the workforce will be alright because the conventional wisdom tells us
so.

However, the picture we have attempted to paint is not one of happy
families watched over by paternalist owners. Rather it is a picture of
autocratic management style, dictated by enormous external pressures on
the owner managers themselves to cut costs. The workforce can no
longer resort to frequent job changing to alleviate the conditions of
work, but equally finds difficulty in undertaking collective action,
except in extreme cases. This difficulty should not, we contend, be
mistaken for harmony; small scale enterprises such as the clothing
firms we have studied have advantages in terms of managerial control,
especially if the workforce is female. They are not necessarily the
'better environment' for the worker envisaged by the Bolton Report.

NOTES

1. The interviews with Managers took place early in 1981. At that time,
   average bonus levels were about £15 per week on top of a basic wage
   of just over £55.

REFERENCES

Barrett, B., Rhodes, E.,Beishon, J. (eds.) *Industrial Relations and the wider Society*, Collier MacMillan, London, 1975.

Becker, G. *Human Capital*, Columbia University Press, 1979.

Berger, S. and Piore, M., *Dualism and Discontinuity in Industrial Societies*, Cambridge University Press, 1980.

Blackburn,R. and Mann, M., *The Working Class in the Labour Market*, MacMillan, London, 1979.

Bolton Report, 1971.

Bosanquet, N. and Doeringer, P., Is there a dual labour market in Great Britain? *Economic Journal*, 1973.

Clothing Manufacturer, The. April 1981.

Curran, J. and Stanworth, J. Worker Involvement and Social Relations in the Small Firm , *The Sociological Review*, Vol.27, No.2, 1979a.

Curran, J. and Stanworth, J. Self selection and the Small Firm worker – a critique and an alternative view , *Sociology*, Vol.13, No.3, 1979b.

Curran, J. and Stanworth, J. Industrial Relations and the Small Firm , paper presented to 3rd UK SBMTA Conference, Manchester, September, 1980.

Curran, J. and Stanworth, J. Size of Workplace and Attitudes to Industrial Relations in the Printing and Electronics Industries , *British Journal of Industrial Relations*, Vol.19, No.1, 1981a.

Curran, J. and Stanworth, J., The Social Dynamics of Small Manufacturing Enterprise , *Journal of Management Studies*, Vol.18, No.2, 1981.

Department of Employment Gazette, January, 1978.

Doeringer, P. and Piore, M., *Internal Labour Markets and Manpower Analysis*, D.C. Heath, 1981.

Edwards, R., *Contested Terrain - the Transformation of the Workplace in the 20th Century*, Heineman, London, 1979.

Elliston Research Associates, Report to Economic Development Committee for the Clothing Industry, NEDO, 1973.

Friedman, A.L. *Industry and Labour*, Macmillan, 1977.

Frobel, F., *The New International Division of Labour*, Cambridge University Press, 1980.

Henderson, J. and Johnson, B., Labour Relations in the Smaller Firm , *Personnel Management*, December, 1974.

Hobsbawn, E. *Labouring Men*, Weidenfeld and Nicholson, 1964.

Howe, Sir Geoffrey, *Employment News*, No.84, May 1981.

Hyman, R., The Politics of Workplace Trade Unionism , *Capital and Class*, Summer 1979.

Ingham, G.K. *Size of Industrial Organisation and Worker Behaviour*, Cambridge University Press, 1970.

177

International Labour Office, *Employment Effects in the Clothing Industry of Changes in International Trade,* ILO, Geneva, 1980.

Kerr, C., 'The Balkanisation of Labour Markets' in Barrett et al, 1975.

Lewis, R. and Steward, R., *The Boss,* Phoenix House, London, 1958.

Marsh, A.E., Evans, E.O. and Garcia P., *Workplace Industrial Relations in Engineering,* Kogan Page (Associates) 1971.

Nash, M., 'Industrial Relations in the Small Firm', *Employee Relations,* Vol.2, No.4, 1980.

Nichols   T. and Beynon, H., *Living with Capitalism,* Routledge and Kegan Paul, 1977.

Pollett, A.,'Resistance and Control', *Socialist Review,* No.13, 1979.

Reich, M., Gordon, D., and Edwards, R., 'Labour Market Segmentation', in Atkinson, A. (ed.), *Wealth, Income and Inequality,* Oxford University Press, 1980.

Rubery, J., 'Structured Labour Markets, Worker Organisation and Low Pay', in Amsden, A. (ed.), *The Economics of Women and Work,* Penguin, 1980.

Schumacher, E.F., *Small is Beautiful,* Bland and Briggs, 1973.

Transport and General Workers Union, 'Textiles and Clothing – the Fight for Survival', 1980.

Trades Union Congress, 'Textiles, Clothing and Footwear - Policies for the Future', 1980.

Turner, H.A., Clark, G., and Roberts, G., *Labour Relations in the Motor Industry,* Geo. Allen and Unwin, 1967.

V GOVERNMENT AND THE SMALL FIRM

Government Aid to the Small Firm Since Bolton
MICHAEL BEESLEY AND PETER WILSON

The Government first recognised that small firms might face problems
and have needs different from those of large firms in the 1960s.   The
appointment of the Bolton Committee in 1969 to investigate the problems
of small firms and to make recommendations signalled the beginnings of
an overt small business policy by Government.   The publication of its
Report in November 1971 promoted an unprecedented interest in the small
business sector, partly through its examination of hypotheses about the
disadvantages widely thought to be suffered by small firms and partly
through its recommendations for remedial action by Government.   Most
of the government measures covered by this paper then began to emerge
and the genesis of public policy towards small business gained momentum.
The growth of concern about small business is evidenced by the increasing volume of statements made by government spokesmen.   Small business
first began to be debated seriously in 1964.   An analysis of entries to
Hansard indicates the growth of Parliamentary interest from its beginnings in the mid-1960s, the perceptible impact of the Bolton Report in
the early 1970s and the subsequent rapid increase in the number of
debates, questions and answers in Parliament, all reflecting a deepening
interest in the contribution of small firms to economic growth and
employment creation and a concern with the impact of government policies
on the health of the sector (Gorb, Dowell and Wilson, 1981: 255).

Before the Bolton Report, assistance to small business was ad hoc,
emerging as a by-product of policies towards industrial efficiency,
training, technology, organisation or location.   The prevailing philosophy at the time of the Bolton Report was one of bigness, exemplified
by an industrial policy of rationalisation and reorganisation into
larger units capable of exploiting supposed economies of scale.   For
instance, the Industrial Reorganisation Corporation (IRC), established

in 1966, was charged with the reorganisation and development of firms
in strategic industries in order to ensure that Britain competed
effectively in world markets where large size was considered a necessary minimum condition for survival and growth.   According to Allen
(1970: 162) the IRC embodied the development of more systematic
government intervention in industrial activity;   although the origins
of this new approach are to be found in the promotion of large-scale
enterprise, in them also lies the simultaneous development of government policy towards small business.

In this paper we describe how government policy and assistance
towards small business have evolved since the late 1940s, but particularly since the Bolton Committee published its findings in 1971.   We
confine our discussion to Britain, although much of the assistance
applies equally to Northern Ireland, which, in addition, has its own
agencies charged with local business development.   The assistance
measures until August 1981 are listed in chronological order by type of
measure in Appendix A.   In the light of our findings, we draw some
tentative conclusions about trends in government policy and assistance
to small business and point to some likely future developments[1].

DEFINITIONS

The problem of definition of a small business is usually resolved by
referring to the Bolton Committee (1971: 1-4) which concluded that a
'small firm' is recognised by three broad qualitative characteristics.
First, a small firm tends to have a relatively small share of its relevant market, implying that it has little or no power to affect either
price, quantity or its environment.   It is possible, however, for a
small firm to have a large share of a small yet specialised market
niche.   Second, a small firm has no formalised management structure;
rather the owner manager is responsible for decision making.   The extent
of formalisation will vary among firms, however, since as the firm
grows, personal owner management is replaced partially or wholly by
professional management.   Third, a small firm is independent of the
control of a parent company, implying a certain freedom to make
decisions.   But even if management is free from interference by a parent
company, it is usually inextricably dependent on its network of

182

advisers, customers, suppliers and bankers. So these attributes are
not necessary conditions for being deemed 'small business', although
most commentators assume they are.

In practice, only close observation will reveal whether the small
business exhibits these characteristics. In fact, the behaviour and
role of the owner manager or entrepreneur are the key to a working
definition. (In small firms, the behaviour of the owner manager and the
behaviour of the firm are synonomous.) But in order to determine changes
in the small firm population over time, numerical definitions are also
necessary. These are given in Appendices B, C and D. Generally,
small firms in manufacturing are defined as those with fewer than 200
employees and in other sectors, a variety of definitions applies.

GOVERNMENT POLICY TOWARDS SMALL BUSINESS

In seeking to establish whether successive British governments have
developed explicit policies towards small business and what the nature
of these policies is, we look to three main indicators of public policy.
These are:

    a) specific small business legislation;

    b) statements made by government spokesmen; and

    c) other general legislation and measures to assist small
      business.

Britain has no specific small business legislation, such as is to be
found in the legislation of other countries, particularly that of the
United States. For instance, the Small Business Act of 1953 which
established the Small Business Administration was the culmination of a
long history of legislation sympathetic to the independent business,
starting with the Sherman Anti-trust Act of 1890 (Bruchey, 1980: 21-23).

Without the benefit of such obvious small business legislation,
evidence must be sought elsewhere. The Bolton Committee, established
by a Labour Government sympathetic to the needs of small business, is an
appropriate starting point. When the Committee published its report of
1971, the Conservative Government welcomed its findings and recommendations and the Secretary of State for Trade and Industry at the time
commented that he was well aware of the place of small firms in the
economy and that he would ensure that 'their interests be taken into

account in the formulation of policies' (Davies, 1971). In June 1972, the Under-Secretary of State with responsibility for small firms, a new position recommended by the Bolton Committee, stated that he was 'determined that small firms should be allowed to flourish and thrive in the freest possible environment, unhampered by unnecessary restrictions and unintentional discrimination' (Grant, 1972).

The Conservative Government acted on many of the Report's recommendations, although it was firmly against discriminatory policies in favour of small firms. It intended, rather, to remove past discrimination and to prevent discrimination being built into new policies, by considering measures necessary for the encouragement of individual enterprise and initiative (Trade and Industry, 1972).

These intentions were largely in sympathy with the Bolton Committee's conclusions that positive discrimination by Government in favour of the small business was unjustified and that the sector could perform its self-regenerative function unaided. It did find that Government had imposed a number of unintentional disabilities on the small business which amounted to discrimination (Bolton Report, 1971: 87-91). We discern a commitment to these sentiments by the Conservative Government, with policies oriented to two objectives: first, providing an environment in which the small firm could thrive, free from interference of any kind; and second, removing the discriminatory impact of existing legislation. Although evidence of the former is not presented here, and indeed would be hard to gather, there is evidence of the removal of discrimination and the exemption of small firms from certain statutory obligations which, it was alleged, bore more heavily on them than on larger firms. We point to this evidence in the following section.

The Labour Government of 1974 adopted the same objectives. The accent was to be on the avoidance and elimination of unintentional discrimination against small firms and the creation of a climate favourable to their growth, including protection from the alleged anti-competitive market practices of the giant companies (Fraser, 1977). In June 1974 the Minister of State for the Department of Industry (DOI) pointed to the Labour Government's 'unambiguous' commitment to an active small business sector, which was 'important in regional terms as a seedbed of regional growth and a source of diversification and balance in the industrial structure' (Heffer, 1974).

The Labour Government's attitude to small firms soon acquired a flavour of more direct support. The Secretary of State for Industry in 1975 signalled a 'more vigorous' policy for small firms because of their local markets, their labour intensiveness and the close relationship between the owner manager and the workforce. Indeed, he claimed to be 'strongly sympathetic' to small firms and 'strongly in favour' of their development (Benn, 1975).

This theme was further developed with the appointment in September 1977 of Lord Lever, a senior Minister in the Labour Government, and Robert Cryer, the Under-Secretary of State in the Department of Industry with responsibility for small firms, to make a special study of their problems and to recommend and initiate remedial action. Increased official concern for small business was clear and implied that existing policies were not adequate. As a result of Lord Lever's study, budget-ary measures were announced in October 1977 and in April 1978 as 'part of a developing policy in which Government was going to show a contin-uous responsiveness to the needs of small firms' (Lever, 1978).

In January 1977 the Government appointed the Wilson Committee to inquire into the role of the financial institutions and the provision of funds for industry and trade, and the Committee's study of the financing of small firms was published in March 1979 (Wilson Committee, 1979). Some of the recommendations of the Committee were subsequently accepted, particularly those involving no apparent change in government policy. Of the recommendations which could be classified as discriminating in favour of small business, the proposals for Small Firm Investment Companies, an English Development Agency and a publicly underwritten loan guarantee scheme were the most extreme, signalling the Government's willingness to depart even further from its adherence to a non-discrim-inatory small business policy. In the event, the loan guarantee scheme and certain investment incentives were introduced, though in a more muted form than that proposed by the Committee; but no Agency has yet been sanctioned.

The Conservative Government of 1979 pursued the trend towards greater intervention in the affairs of small business started by the previous Labour Government. The Under-Secretary of State responsible for small firms stated in July 1980:

'There is a recognition on both sides of the House of the
importance of small businesses as the seedcorn from which
wealth creation and many jobs in the future will come.
We have far too few such businesses. We need many more.
The balance between the incentives to start a business,
the hurdles which face those who start and the burdens
they have to carry has been tipped so far that the logical
person has not felt it worthwhile to start a business.

The Government are engaged in a threefold task. The first
is to identify the burdens and to pull them down, to identify
the hurdles and take them away, so that it is easier for
people to start. Secondly, we have to increase incentives
for them to do so. Thirdly, we have to look at the problems
of financing those who have started, or are seeking to start,
in terms of the money inside the business as well as
incentive in terms of what one can take out in reward for
success' (Mitchell, 1980).

We recognise in this statement the familiar references to the removal
of discrimination. But for the first time a government spokesman also
spoke of a need to encourage the birth of small firms (as opposed to
their survival and growth) and to do so directly. Not only were incentives mentioned as an element of policy, but the allusion to the
problems of financing new and small firms presaged further direct preferential assistance by Government. Although the Bolton Committee had
expressed concern about the low birthrate of new firms, successive
Governments had introduced few measures specifically oriented to new
firms. Nevertheless there has been a consistent increase in the numbers
of new businesses since 1974 and a clear upward trend in these numbers
since the mid-1960s (Gorb, Dowell and Wilson, 1981: 261). Policy has
changed simultaneously with this increase.

In spite of this revealed change of direction over the last few years,
government spokesmen still do not espouse a policy of direct preferential
assistance. For instance, in March 1981 the Under-Secretary of State
for small firms reiterated the Government's policy of removing obstacles
and burdens and changing the overall climate in which the small business
operated (McGregor, 1981). There was no allusion to direct preferential
assistance. Yet the Business Opportunities Programme was launched by

186

the Government in May 1981, following the measures introduced in the
1981 Finance Act, another example of direct encouragement of small
business. The Programme's emphasis on raising national awareness of
the opportunities and rewards of small business adds a new dimension to
government policy: in order to stimulate the birth of more new
ventures, the Government is pursuing an aggressive marketing campaign
throughout the country.

In July 1981 the Chief Secretary to the Treasury outlined four
elements of industrial policy, namely the reduction of inflation,
'supply side' policies to improve market efficiency, privatisation and
market-orientation of the public sector and support for industry in
selected areas. It was intended to stimulate the economy by removing
constraints to the efficient operation of market forces and by improving
incentives to enterprise and rewards for effort, including the introduction of measures to stimulate the growth of small business (Brittan,
1981).

GOVERNMENT AID

In this section, we confine ourselves to general comments about the
nature and extent of government assistance; individual measures are
listed in Appendix A. With the exclusion of assistance that has either
a marginal or no effective bearing on small firms at all, it is possible
to identify three groups of measures and within these, a number of sub-
groups.

These three groups also mark the three periods of government activity
noted below. The first from 1946 to 1960, covers the period when there
was no specific assistance to small business. The second period up to
1970, was characterised by government measures to remove discrimination.
The third period covers the measures introduced since the publication of
the Bolton Report, including most instances of positive discrimination.
This period can be further sub-divided into two five year periods, and
a perceptible increase in the number of direct measures is recorded in
the latter period. Each type of activity, with varying incidence, has
been continuous, once commenced.

The first group consists of those measures that indirectly or inadvertently have a significant effect on small business, despite their intended universal application. These are listed in Appendix A. They can be further grouped into regional or locational assistance, such as the Scottish and Welsh Development Agencies which have their own small business units; assistance with production efficiency, training and advice, such as the Industrial Training Boards; technological assistance as with the National Research Development Corporation; and assistance consistent with economic policy, as with industry aid under the Industry Act of 1972. Until 1976 there was no marked trend in indirect assistance although in the last five years there has been a perceptible increase over the earlier period, which as we illustrate in Appendix A has been characteristic of all government assistance to small business.

Most indirect assistance falls into the regional assistance sub-group and the bulk of this has been introduced since 1970. A substantial amount of assistance under the Industry Act has been directed to small firms and local authorities have also begun to orientate their employment policies increasingly towards small business, which effectively gives small business policy a greater regional and local dimension (Wilson, 1980). Indeed pressures brought to bear by local government organisations on central Government to devolve additional small business powers down to the local level are intense; many local authorities are considering directly investing in small businesses through local enterprise trusts set up for this purpose (Windass, 1981).

The introduction of training and advisory assistance, although directed at industry as a whole, can have a considerable impact on small business. This has been recognised by successive Governments, culminating in a more direct approach in recent years. The recognition that small firms are at a particular disadvantage in the market for training and advice is based on the limitations of the owner manager with regard to personnel training expertise. Although such expertise is available externally in appropriate amounts, for most very small firms it would still be uneconomical to employ it. Despite the availability of industrial training and advice from the public sector at subsidised rates, small firms have not been successfully absorbed into training schemes.

The Removal of Discrimination

The second group has been imposed to remove discrimination against small
firms, largely by exempting them from various statutory obligations.
It is based on the proposition that management resources in the owner
managed small firm are lumpy: they consist essentially of one person.
To add to them involves a disproportionately large increment, not
easily achieved. The small firm, on this view, is placed at a considerable disadvantage relative to larger firms with respect to any given
commitment requiring managerial attention. Large companies need only
make relatively small adjustments in resources to deal with the duties
and obligations imposed on industry and commerce by the Government.

Within this group are three distinct sub-groups. Regional exemptions
cover industrial and commercial construction allowances to small firms;
administrative exemptions such as disclosure exemptions under the
Companies Act and the revision of statistical surveys of small firms;
and exemption under economic and social policy, particularly the recognition that the smallest firms should have reduced responsibilities
in relation to dismissal procedures under the Employment Act.

Direct Preferential Assistance

The third group of measures discriminates specifically or positively in
favour of small business by providing resources and inducements. The
majority of measures fall into this category, most being introduced
after 1971 with a clear upward trend in the last five years. Direct
assistance since the Conservative Government came to power in 1979 has
accelerated further, despite the claim that such positive discrimination
was never to be incorporated into government policy.

It is possible to distinguish three broad types of assistance within
this group. The first type is designed to further the general aims of
economic and social policy and consists of measures to promote exports,
particularly among small first time exporters, rural development,
regional assistance and technological change. The second type is designed to favour small firms per se and consists of non-financial aid

189

such as training and advisory services and the Small Firms Division of the Department of Industry, charged with overall responsibility for the sector. The third type consists of financial measures such as fiscal incentives to establish new ventures, increasing the rewards due to entrepreneurial activity, improving the supply of venture capital to new firms and providing a loan guarantee scheme for loans made by the private sector banks./ We observe two main features relating to these financial measures. The first is the marked increase in direct financial measures relative to other direct measures over the last few years; and the second, the focus on new ventures relative to establish- ed small firms.

SUMMARY AND COMMENT: FUTURE DEVELOPMENTS IN PUBLIC POLICY

The large number of measures listed in the appendices confirms that since 1946 there has been continuing government interest in small business. But until the 1960s assistance tended to be ad hoc, incident- al and indirect. Thereafter, increasing official concern with small business was reflected in the introduction of direct preferential treat- ment - more than 75 per cent of government measures are either direct or related to the removal of discrimination. Over two-thirds of all measures have been introduced since 1970 and over one-third since 1975. A notable feature of government assistance is the orientation to manu- facturing.   Only one-third of assistance is orientated to non-manu- facturing, reflecting the concern with the declining share of manufact- uring in the economy.

The trend to greater direct assistance is likely to continue unabated. In the period 1946-70, 53 per cent of all measures introduced were direct, while in the period 1971-81 this proportion was 64 per cent, rising to 72 per cent in the five year period up to 1981. Successive Governments have implemented a de facto policy increasingly favourable to small business and the introduction of further measures that actively discriminate in its favour is possible. As an indication of future developments, the following policy related issues and assistance are likely to concern small business in the medium term. These fall into the categories economic and social policy, regional assistance, govern- ment procurement, industrial deconcentration and legislative consolida- tion.)

Based on the trends in small business policy observed above as well as
on issues, currently neglected, which are beginning to attract attention, we can identify at least three areas of likely future activity.
The first is further support for the introduction of advanced technology in small firms and the encouragement of advanced technology output
by small firms, either through indirect assistance by the British
Technology Group or through direct financial assistance and incentives.
The new role for the National Enterprise Board as a catalyst in the
promotion of advanced technology and small firms is likely to be
further strengthened.

The second area is the promotion of co-operative enterprise through
the Co-operative Development Agency and the Industrial Common Ownership
Movement. Although the present Conservative Government is not disposed
to encouraging co-operatives through preferential support, the opposition Labour Party and Labour-controlled local authorities have expressed
their strong support for co-operatives. Similarly there is likely to
be increased support for community business ventures.

The third area is the encouragement of minority-owned enterprise.
While there is currently no specific assistance in this area, the
attention of central and local government is increasingly being drawn
to minority businesses (Home Affairs Committee, 1980). The rioting
and general unrest experienced in 1981 have emphasised the special circumstances prevailing in areas occupied by minority groups, particularly
those of West Indian origin. The deprivation and disadvantages alleg-
edly suffered by small businesses owned by these minorities are likely
to attract remedial assistance, principally from local authorities.

Regional Assistance

The further orientation of regional investment incentives and other
assistance away from large to small firms is the likely consequence of
the continued structural decline of some of Britain's older industries.
Also the emphasis on the employment creation impact of small, rather
than large, firms will tend to strengthen the flow of assistance to the
former in the assisted areas and in nominated inner city areas (Storey,

1980). (The introduction of Enterprise Zones in the 1980 Finance Act provides a further channel for more direct assistance. Enterprise Zones are designed to attract industry into pockets of inner city need by offering a range of financial and other inducements, including greater flexibility in terms of planning regulations. Measures to assist specifically small firms could at a later stage be introduced alongside existing Enterprise Zone incentives.)

As we have pointed out earlier, there has been an increasing flow of resources to small business at the local level through local authorities and intermediary agencies in which both central and local government are indirectly involved. The Association of Metropolitan Authorities for instance, has already called for greater powers at the local authority level to intervene directly in the establishment and growth of small firms. In London the proposed founding of a Greater London Enterprise Board, charged specifically with the development of new and small businesses, is evidence of the continuing trend to greater local intervention in the affairs of small business.

Government Procurement

Central and local government, the nationalised industries and quasi-government bodies provide a large untapped resource for exploitation by small firms in the form of procurement contracts. The Bolton Committee noted that certain government departments were unintentionally favouring large firms when placing procurement contracts (Bolton, 1971: 80), and recommended that purchasing policies be investigated by the Small Firms Division with a view to increasing the flow of products and services provided by small firms to the Government[2].) A possible extension of a passive interest in the share of government contracts going to small firms is the system adopted in the United States whereby a minimum proportion of these contracts is guaranteed for small firms.

Policy has not proceeded this far. However, the present Government has stated that the flow of information to small firms about procurement contracts should be improved (Hansard, 1979a). To this end, the Small Firms Information Centres have produced a booklet on government procurement, while senior Ministers in all government departments have been questioned about their respective procurement activities (Hansard,

1979b).

Industrial Deconcentration

A further source of possible developments in policy is a coincidence of
arguments in favour of small scale organisation, growing in popular
appeal, and the specific need of large firms to shed labour in response
to economic recession, to make profit centres more responsive to the
business and social environment and to accentuate entrepreneurial initiative. The activities of such nationalised industries as the
British Steel Corporation in assisting small firms are only one step
removed from hiving off certain production tasks into subcontract work,
where executives and/or skilled workers might take severance or redundancy pay and start up a new enterprise supplying their former employers
with the necessary administrative, managerial and other assistance
provided by the parent company. Large private companies could, it is
argued, be persuaded to act in a similar fashion where there were clear
economic and social benefits, or where redundancies were inevitable at
management and artisan levels. In these cases, tax incentives or tax
holidays could be offered if benefits were clearly visible.

Consolidating Legislation and Small Business Representation

Although the introduction of a wide range of additional measures to
assist small business cannot be discounted as part of the likely future
direction of government policy, the current diversity and complexity of
assistance described in this article are reaching a point where consol-
idating legislation for small firms is indicated. The plethora of
assistance also raises the question of a national agency charged with
representing small business at all levels of the public and private
sectors (Bannock, 1981: 123). The Small Firms Division, based as it is
in the Department of Industry, cannot easily perform this role. But no
commitment by Government to a new institution has yet appeared.

A.   INDIRECT ASSISTANCE

1946-1960

- A1   National Research Development Corporation
  (1948, manufacturing)[3]
- A2   British Productivity Council (1952, manufacturing)

1961-1970

- A3   Industrial Training Boards (1964)
- A4   Highlands and Islands Development Board
  (1965, retailing and services excluded)

1971-1981

- A5   Industry Assistance (1972, manufacturing)
- A6   Local Authority Assistance (1972, mainly manufacturing)
- A7   Scottish Development Agency (1975)
- A8   Welsh Development Agency (1976)
- A9   Development Board for Rural Wales (1976)
- A10 National Enterprise Board (1978, manufacturing)
- A11 European Investment Bank (1978, manufacturing)

B.   THE REMOVAL OF DISCRIMINATION

1961-1970

- B1   Industrial Development Certificates (1962)
- B2   Office Development Permits (1965)
- B3   Companies Act Disclosure (1967)

1971-1981

- B4   Employment Legislation (1971)
- B5   Value Added Tax (1972)
- B6   Price Code (1973)
- B7   Collection of Statistics (1973)
- B8   Competition Policy (1980)

C. DIRECT PREFERENTIAL ASSISTANCE

I. Economic and Social Policy

1961-1970

C1   Small Exporters Policy (1961, manufacturing)

C2   Low Cost Automation Centres (1961, manufacturing)

C3   Council for Small Industries in Rural Areas
(1968, manufacturing, services and tourism)

C4   Export Award (1969, manufacturing)

1971-1981

C5   Crafts Advisory Committee (1971, manufacturing)

C6   Export Educational Visits (1974)

C7   Co-operatives & Common Ownerships (1976)

C8   Small Firms Employment Subsidy (1977, manufacturing)

C9   Computer Aided Production Management (1977, manufacturing)

C10 Market Entry Guarantee Scheme (1978, manufacturing)

C11 Business Opportunities Programme (1981)

II. Non-Financial Direct Assistance

1961-1970

C12 Industrial Liaison Service (1961, manufacturing)

C13 Production Engineering Advisory Service (1967, manufacturing)

C14 Consultancy Scheme (1968, manufacturing)

1971-1981

C15 Small Firms Division (1971)

C16 Small Firms Information Centres (1973)

C17 Small Firms Counselling Service (1976)

C18 Collaborative Arrangements (1976)

C19 Management Education (1976)

C20 Manufacturing Advisory Service (1977, manufacturing)

C21 Small Factory Units (1977)

III. Financial Direct Assistance

1961-1970

C22 Capital Gains Tax (1965)

C23 Corporation Tax (1972)

C24 Close Companies (1972)

C25 Rating Relief (1974, retailing and services)

C26 Capital Transfer Tax (1975)

C27 National Health Service Dispensing (1978, retailing)

C28 Income Tax (1978)

C29 Loan Guarantee Scheme (1981)

SUMMARY OF ASSISTANCE: Number of Measures per Period

1946–1960	:	2
1961–1965	:	8
1966–1970	:	5
1971–1975	:	15
1976–1981	:	18

APPENDIX B   STATISTICAL DEFINITIONS OF SMALL BUSINESS

Industry   Definition (upper limits)[4]

Industry	Definition (upper limits)[4]
Manufacturing	200 employees
Retailing	£185,000 p.a. turnover
Wholesale Trade	£730,000 p.a. turnover
Construction	25 employees
Mining and Quarrying	25 employees
Motor Trade	£365,000 p.a. turnover
Miscellaneous Services	£185,000 p.a. turnover
Road Transport	5 vehicles
Catering	All except multiples and brewery managed public houses

APPENDIX C   SPECIFIC DEFINITIONS RELATING TO GOVERNMENT
ASSISTANCE

Type of Assistance	Definition (upper limits)
1. Definitions relating to employment	
EIB loans	500 employees
Proprietory company (proposed)	50 employees
Employment Act exemptions	20 employees
CoSIRA aid	20 employees (skilled)
Export award	200 employees
Export visits	200 employees
Employment subsidy	200 employees
Computer Aided Production Management	500 employees
Industrial Liaison Service	500 employees
Consultancy Scheme	500 employees (min. 25)
Collaborative Arrangements	200 employees (manufacturing)
Manufacturing Advisory Service	1,000 employees (min. 100)
2. Definitions relating to annual turnover	
Companies Act disclosure exemption	£1 million
Proprietory company (proposed)	£1.3 million
VAT registration	£15,000
Price Code exemptions	£1 million (manufacturing)
	£250,000 (distribution, services)
	£100,000 (professions)
Competition Act exemptions	£5 million
3. Miscellaneous definitions	
EIB loans	£20 million (fixed assets)
IDC exemption	50,000 square feet
ODP exemption	30,000 square feet
Proprietory company (proposed)	£650,000 (bal. sheet total)
Small Exporter Policy	£100,000 (export value)
Corporation Tax reduced rate	£80,000 (profits)

Type of Assistance	Lower Limit	Upper Limit
Highland Venture Capital (HIDB)	£25,000	£300,000
Industry Aid	£10,000	–
WDA Small Business Unit Loans	–	£50,000
WDA loan guarantee scheme	–	£50,000
DBRW loans	–	£30,000
Newtown Securities (NEB)	£5,000	£25,000
Sapling Enterprises (NEB)	£50,000	–
Oakwood (NEB)	–	£50,000
EIB loans	£15,000	£2.5 mil.
CoSIRA loans	–	£50,000
Market Entry Guarantee Scheme	£20,000	£100,000
Loan Guarantee Scheme	–	£75,000

NOTES

1. A more detailed account of government assistance can be found in Gorb, Dowell and Wilson, 1981: 271–302.

2. Public sector buying power ammounted to £22,000 million in 1980 (The Times, 12 January 1981).

3. Year refers to year of inception; manufacturing refers to industry coverage; where no industry is mentioned, the assistance applies to all, or most, industries.

4. Limits have been revised upwards since the Bolton Commission originally published these definitions. Figures are at 1978 prices. (Interim Report of the Committee to Review the Functioning of Financial Institutions op.cit. p.43).

REFERENCES

Allen, G.C., *The Structure of Industry in Britain*, Longman, 1970.

Bannock, G., *The Economics of Small Firms*, Basil Blackwell, 1981.

Benn, Tony, *Trade and Industry*, Vol.18, No.9, 28 February 1975.

Brittan, Leon, *British Business*, Vol.5, No.13, 24 July 1981.

Bruchey, S.W., (ed.), *Small Business in American Life*, Columbia University Press, 1980.

Davies, John, *Hansard*, Col.188, Vol.825, 3 November, 1971.

Financing of Small Firms (The), Interim Report of the Committee to Review the Functioning of Financial Institutions, Cmnd.7503, HMSO, 1979 (The Wilson Report).

Fraser, John, *Trade and Industry*, Vol.29, No.4, 28 October 1977.

Gorb, P., Dowell, P.,and Wilson P., (eds.), *Small Business Perspectives*, Armstrong Publishing, 1981.

Grant, Anthony, *Hansard*, Col.1061, Vol.838, 12 June 1972.

Hansard (a). Col.128, Vol.965, 27 March 1979.

Hansard (b). Col.700, Vol.973, 13 November 1979.

Heffer, Eric, *Trade and Industry*, Vol.18, No.9, 21 April 1978.

Home Affairs Committee, House of Commons, *Racial Disadvantage: West Indians in Business in Britain*, HMSO, 1980.

Lever, Harold, *Trade and Industry*, Vol.31, No.3, 21 April 1978.

McGregor, John, *British Business*, Vol.4, No.11, 13 March 1981.

Mitchell, David, *Hansard*, Col.1553, Vol.989, 30 July 1980.

Small Firms - Report of the Committee of Inquiry on Small Firms, Cmnd. 4811, HMSO, 1971 (The Bolton Report).

Storey, D.J., Small firms and the regional problem, *The Banker*, Vol.130, No.657, November 1980.

Trade and Industry, Vol.8, No.2, 13 July 1972.

Wilson, P., *Local Authority Assistance to Small Business*, Conference paper, UK Small Business Management Teachers Association, Manchester Business School, September 1980.

Windass, S., (ed.), *Local Initiatives in Great Britain*, Foundation for Alternatives, 1981.